ON THE INCARNATION

ON THE INCARNATION

THE TREATISE
De Incarnatione Verbi Dei

ST ATHANASIUS

Translated and edited by A Religious of C.S.M.V.

With an Introduction by
C. S. LEWIS

New Edition, revised, with a letter of St Athanasius
On the Interpretation of the Psalms added as an Appendix

ST VLADIMIR'S SEMINARY PRESS
CRESTWOOD, NEW YORK

Library of Congress Cataloging-in-Publication Data

Athanasius, Saint, Patriarch of Alexandria, d. 373
　[De incarnatione, English]
　On the incarnation: the treatise De incarnatione Verbi Dei / St Athanasius;
translated and edited by a religious of C.S.M.V.; with an introduction by C.S.
Lewis.
　　p. cm.
　"New edition, revised, with a letter of St. Athanasius on the interpretation of
the Psalms added as an appendix."
Included bibliographical references.
　ISBN 0-913836-40-0 (alk. paper)
　I. Incarnation—early works to 1800.　I. Title.
BR65.A443D4I3　　　　1996　　　　　　　　　　　　　　96-26145
232'.1—dc20　　　　　　　　　　　　　　　　　　　　　CIP

This edition first published in the USA in 1993 by

ST VLADIMIR'S SEMINARY PRESS

575 Scarsdale Road, Crestwood, NY 10707
1-800-204-2665

Original edition published in 1944 by Centenary Press.
American Edition published in 1946 by the MacMillan Company.
First published by A.R.Mowbray & Co., Ltd., England, in a Second and
Revised Edition, with Appendix, in 1953.

ISBN 0-913836-40-0

INTRODUCTION

THERE is a strange idea abroad that in every subject the ancient books should be read only by the professionals, and that the amateur should content himself with the modern books. Thus I have found as a tutor in English Literature that if the average student wants to find out something about Platonism, the very last thing he thinks of doing is to take a translation of Plato off the library shelf and read the *Symposium*. He would rather read some dreary modern book ten times as long, all about "isms" and influences and only once in twelve pages telling him what Plato actually said. The error is rather an amiable one, for it springs from humility. The student is half afraid to meet one of the great philosophers face to face. He feels himself inadequate and thinks he will not understand him. But if he only knew, the great man, just because of his greatness, is much more intelligible than his modern commentator. The simplest student will be able to understand, if not all, yet a very great deal of what Plato said; but hardly anyone can understand some modern books on Platonism. It has always therefore been one of my main endeavours as a teacher to persuade the young that first-hand knowledge is not only more worth acquiring than second-hand knowledge, but is usually much easier and more delightful to acquire.

This mistaken preference for the modern books and this shyness of the old ones is nowhere more rampant than in theology. Wherever you find a little study circle of Christian laity you can be almost certain that they are studying not St. Luke or St. Paul or St. Augustine or Thomas Aquinas or Hooker or Butler, but M. Berdyaev or M. Maritain or M. Niebuhr or Miss Sayers or even myself.

Now this seems to me topsy-turvy. Naturally, since I myself am a writer, I do not wish the ordinary reader to read no modern books. But if he must read only the new or only the old, I would advise him to read the old. And I would give him this advice precisely because he is an amateur and therefore much less protected than the expert against the dangers of an exclusive contemporary diet. A new book is still on its trial and the amateur is not in a position to judge it. It has to be tested against the great body of Christian thought down the ages, and all its hidden implications (often unsuspected by the author himself) have to be brought to light. Often it cannot be fully understood without the knowledge of a good many other modern books. If you join at eleven o'clock a conversation which began at eight you will often not see the real bearing of what is said. Remarks which seem to you very ordinary will produce laughter or irritation and you will not see why—the reason, of course, being that the earlier stages of the conversation have given them a special point. In the same way sentences in a modern book which look quite ordinary may be directed "at" some other book; in this way you may be led to accept what you would have indignantly rejected if you knew its real significance. The only safety is to have a standard of plain, central Christianity ("mere Christianity" as Baxter called it) which puts the controversies of the moment in their proper perspective. Such a standard can be acquired only from the old books. It is a good rule, after reading a new book, never to allow yourself another new one till you have read an old one in between. If that is too much for you, you should at least read one old one to every three new ones.

Every age has its own outlook. It is specially good at seeing certain truths and specially liable to make certain mistakes. We all, therefore, need the books that will correct the characteristic mistakes of our own period.

4

And that means the old books. All contemporary writers share to some extent the contemporary outlook—even those, like myself, who seem most opposed to it. Nothing strikes me more when I read the controversies of past ages than the fact that both sides were usually assuming without question a good deal which we should now absolutely deny. They thought that they were as completely opposed as two sides could be, but in fact they were all the time secretly united—united *with* each other and *against* earlier and later ages—by a great mass of common assumptions. We may be sure that the characteristic blindness of the twentieth century—the blindness about which posterity will ask, "But how *could* they have thought that?"—lies where we have never suspected it, and concerns something about which there is untroubled agreement between Hitler and President Roosevelt or between Mr. H. G. Wells and Karl Barth. None of us can fully escape this blindness, but we shall certainly increase it, and weaken our guard against it, if we read only modern books. Where they are true they will give us truths which we half knew already. Where they are false they will aggravate the error with which we are already dangerously ill. The only palliative is to keep the clean sea breeze of the centuries blowing through our minds, and this can be done only by reading old books. Not, of course, that there is any magic about the past. People were no cleverer then than they are now; they made as many mistakes as we. But not the *same* mistakes. They will not flatter us in the errors we are already committing; and their own errors, being now open and palpable, will not endanger us. Two heads are better than one, not because either is infallible, but because they are unlikely to go wrong in the same direction. To be sure, the books of the future would be just as good a corrective as the books of the past, but unfortunately we cannot get at them.

5

I myself was first led into reading the Christian classics, almost accidentally, as a result of my English studies. Some, such as Hooker, Herbert, Traherne, Taylor and Bunyan, I read because they are themselves great English writers; others, such as Boethius, St. Augustine, Thomas Aquinas and Dante, because they were "influences." George Macdonald I had found for myself at the age of sixteen and never wavered in my allegiance, though I tried for a long time to ignore his Christianity. They are, you will note, a mixed bag, representative of many Churches, climates and ages. And that brings me to yet another reason for reading them. The divisions of Christendom are undeniable and are by some of these writers most fiercely expressed. But if any man is tempted to think—as one might be tempted who read only contemporaries—that "Christianity" is a word of so many meanings that it means nothing at all, he can learn beyond all doubt, by stepping out of his own century, that this is not so. Measured against the ages "mere Christianity" turns out to be no insipid interdenominational transparency, but something positive, self-consistent, and inexhaustible. I know it, indeed, to my cost. In the days when I still hated Christianity, I learned to recognise, like some all too familiar smell, that almost unvarying *something* which met me, now in Puritan Bunyan, now in Anglican Hooker, now in Thomist Dante. It was there (honeyed and floral) in François de Sales; it was there (grave and homely) in Spenser and Walton; it was there (grim but manful) in Pascal and Johnson; there again, with a mild, frightening, Paradisial flavour, in Vaughan and Boehme and Traherne. In the urban sobriety of the eighteenth century one was not safe—Law and Butler were two lions in the path. The supposed "Paganism" of the Elizabethans could not keep it out; it lay in wait where a man might have supposed himself safest, in the very centre of *The Faerie Queene* and the *Arcadia*. It was,

6

of course, varied; and yet—after all—so unmistakably the same; recognisable, not to be evaded, the odour which is death to us until we allow it to become life:

> an air that kills
> From yon far country blows.

We are all rightly distressed, and ashamed also, at the divisions of Christendom. But those who have always lived within the Christian fold may be too easily dispirited by them. They are bad, but such people do not know what it looks like from without. Seen from there, what is left intact despite all the divisions, still appears (as it truly is) an immensely formidable unity. I know, for I saw it; and well our enemies know it. That unity any of us can find by going out of his own age. It is not enough, but it is more than you had thought till then. Once you are well soaked in it, if you then venture to speak, you will have an amusing experience. You will be thought a Papist when you are actually reproducing Bunyan, a Pantheist when you are quoting Aquinas, and so forth. For you have now got on to the great level viaduct which crosses the ages and which looks so high from the valleys, so low from the mountains, so narrow compared with the swamps, and so broad compared with the sheep-tracks.

The present book is something of an experiment. The translation is intended for the world at large, not only for theological students. If it succeeds, other translations of other great Christian books will presumably follow. In one sense, of course, it is not the first in the field. Translations of the *Theologia Germanica*, the *Imitation*, the *Scale of Perfection*, and the *Revelations* of Lady Julian of Norwich, are already on the market, and are very valuable, though some of them are not very scholarly. But it will be noticed that these are all books of devotion rather than of doctrine. Now the layman or amateur needs to be

7

instructed as well as to be exhorted. In this age his need for knowledge is particularly pressing. Nor would I admit any sharp division between the two kinds of book. For my own part I tend to find the doctrinal books often more helpful in devotion than the devotional books, and I rather suspect that the same experience may await many others. I believe that many who find that "nothing happens" when they sit down, or kneel down, to a book of devotion, would find that the heart sings unbidden while they are working their way through a tough bit of theology with a pipe in their teeth and a pencil in their hand.

This is a good translation of a very great book. St. Athanasius has suffered in popular estimation from a certain sentence in the "Athanasian Creed." I will not labour the point that that work is not exactly a creed and was not by St. Athanasius, for I think it is a very fine piece of writing. The words "Which Faith except every one do keep whole and undefiled, without doubt he shall perish everlastingly" are the offence. They are commonly misunderstood. The operative word is *keep*; not *acquire*, or even *believe*, but *keep*. The author, in fact, is not talking about unbelievers, but about deserters, not about those who have never heard of Christ, nor even those who have misunderstood and refused to accept Him, but of those who having really understood and really believed, then allow themselves, under the sway of sloth or of fashion or any other invited confusion to be drawn away into sub-Christian modes of thought. They are a warning against the curious modern assumption that all changes of belief, however brought about, are necessarily exempt from blame. But this is not my immediate concern. I mention "the creed (commonly called) of St. Athanasius" only to get out of the reader's way what may have been a bogey and to put the true Athanasius in its place. His epitaph is *Athanasius*

8

contra mundum, "Athanasius against the world." We are proud that our own country has more than once stood against the world. Athanasius did the same. He stood for the Trinitarian doctrine, "whole and undefiled," when it looked as if all the civilised world was slipping back from Christianity into the religion of Arius—into one of those "sensible" synthetic religions which are so strongly recommended to-day and which, then as now, included among their devotees many highly cultivated clergymen. It is his glory that he did not move with the times; it is his reward that he now remains when those times, as all times do, have moved away.

When I first opened his *De Incarnatione* I soon discovered by a very simple test that I was reading a masterpiece. I knew very little Christian Greek except that of the New Testament and I had expected difficulties. To my astonishment I found it almost as easy as Xenophon; and only a master mind could, in the fourth century, have written so deeply on such a subject with such classical simplicity. Every page I read confirmed this impression. His approach to the Miracles is badly needed to-day, for it is the final answer to those who object to them as "arbitrary and meaningless violations of the laws of Nature." They are here shown to be rather the re-telling in capital letters of the same message which Nature writes in her crabbed cursive hand; the very operations one would expect of Him who was so full of life that when He wished to die He had to "borrow death from others." The whole book, indeed, is a picture of the Tree of Life— a sappy and golden book, full of buoyancy and confidence. We cannot, I admit, appropriate all its confidence to-day. We cannot point to the high virtue of Christian living and the gay, almost mocking courage of Christian martyrdom, as a proof of our doctrines with quite that assurance which Athanasius takes as a matter of course. But whoever may be to blame for that it is not Athanasius.

9

The translator knows so much more Christian Greek than I that it would be out of place for me to praise her version. But it seems to me to be in the right tradition of English translation. I do not think the reader will find here any of that sawdusty quality which is so common in modern renderings from the ancient languages. That is as much as the English reader will notice; those who compare the version with the original will be able to estimate how much wit and talent is presupposed in such a choice, for example, as "these wiseacres" on the very first page.

C. S. LEWIS.

Contents

	PAGE
INTRODUCTION	3
TRANSLATOR'S PREFACE . . .	13
THE LIFE OF ST. ATHANASIUS . . .	17

THE INCARNATION OF THE WORD OF GOD

CHAPTER

I. CREATION AND THE FALL	25
II. THE DIVINE DILEMMA AND ITS SOLUTION IN THE INCARNATION	31
III. THE DIVINE DILEMMA AND ITS SOLUTION IN THE INCARNATION—*continued* . .	37
IV. THE DEATH OF CHRIST	48
V. THE RESURRECTION	56
VI. REFUTATION OF THE JEWS . . .	64
VII. REFUTATION OF THE GENTILES . .	75
VIII. REFUTATION OF THE GENTILES—*continued* .	83
IX. CONCLUSION	95
APPENDIX: THE LETTER OF ST. ATHANASIUS TO MARCELLINUS ON THE INTERPRETATION OF THE PSALMS	97

11

Translator's Preface to the Second Edition

THIS translation of the *De Incarnatione* of St. Athanasius was made originally with intent to bring that classic of the fourth century within the reach of ordinary Christians at the present day. The method followed in it, therefore, was that which Dr. Moffatt has employed with such effect in dealing with St. Paul's Epistles; that is to say, the long Greek sentences were mostly simplified, paraphrase rather than direct translation was used in a few places to make the meaning clear, and in some others, where the Greek was wordy, the English was slightly condensed. Further, the whole treatise was divided into chapters of modern length, though the sectional divisions of the text, which appear to date from the Benedictine edition of 1698, were retained in the margin. Biblical references were given only where the quotations tallied exactly with our English versions; they were omitted where the Septuagint, which alone St. Athanasius knew, differed from the Massoretic Hebrew upon which our versions rest. Very few other notes were given, because annotation can easily become a hindrance rather than a help, and the modern reader should approach the mystery of Christ as St. Athanasius himself did, "not as a theologian, but as a believing soul in need of a Saviour."[1]

In the nine years since its first appearance, however, this translation seems to have been used as much by students as by those who have no academic interest. But though no other English version is at present available, those for whom St. Athanasius' "golden treatise" is a set book for examination must continue to look else-

[1] Robertson: Introduction to St. Athanasius in *The Nicene and Post Nicene Fathers*.

13

where for any sort of learned commentary on it. In this second edition there are no more notes than in the first; and the only important alterations in the text concern the noun ἐπιδημία and its corresponding verb ἐπιδημέω. The former, so the late Dom Gregory Dix informs us,[1] is the regular Egyptian word for the Incarnation; originally an *epidēmia* meant the state entry of a governor into his province, and it was used also of the "appearances" of pagan gods. He himself translates it as "advent"; and in the nine passages where one or other word occurs in the *De Incarnatione* I have now put "advent" for the noun, in place of "sojourn" in the first edition, and "come" instead of "dwell" for the verb.

As an Appendix to the *De Incarnatione* we print now the *Epistola ad Marcellinum*, which was first published separately in 1949 under the title *St. Athanasius on the Psalms*. This letter bears no date, nor is there any external reference by which to fix it. But two pieces of internal evidence suggest that, like the *De Incarnatione*, it was a work of St. Athanasius' youth. One of these is the frequent reference to persecution as a normal element in Christian life, which after 313 it ceased to be; and the other is the absence of reference to the Arian heresy, which first reared its ugly head in 319. Alternatively, the saint may have written the letter as a leisure product during one of his five exiles for the Faith between 335 and 366. It makes no difference. Whenever written, *Ad Marcellinum* is a window on to a very holy soul; and it shows us also how Christians used the Psalter, both in their private and in their corporate worship, at a time when the Divine Office existed only in embryo and even the Liturgy was only beginning to take shape.

The *De Incarnatione* was translated from Dr. F. L. Cross's edition of the text, published by S.P.C.K. in

[1] Dix: *The Shape of the Liturgy* (pub. 1943), p. 163, note.

14

1939; the *Epistola ad Marcellinum* was done by comparing the Benedictine edition of 1698 (most kindly lent by Dr. Cross) with the text given in Migne's *Patrologia Graeca*, Vol. 27. The latter is based on an Alexandrian MS unknown to the earlier editor, and is usually the better; but even so there are some passages where the text as it stands can hardly be correct. The apparent meaning is brought out by paraphrase where this occurs; and throughout the letter I have substituted the familiar English-Hebrew numbering of the Psalms for that of the Septuagint, though it is always the Greek text that is translated.

My very grateful thanks are due again to Dr. Cross, to our former Chaplain the Reverend G. B. Enders, and to three of our Sisters, one of whom is now in Paradise, for help and encouragement over one or both translations between 1942 and 1948; and also to Mr. C. S. Lewis for the delightful Introduction that is reprinted here. And behind these recent debts my gratitude goes out to my former tutor, the late Dr. B. J. Kidd, sometime Warden of Keble and for twenty-one years also Warden of C.S.M.V., who over forty years ago first fired me with love and reverence for the saint who saved the Catholic Faith.

WANTAGE, *January* 1953.

THE LIFE OF ST. ATHANASIUS

EVERY student of Church History in the fourth century knows that it was St. Athanasius who, in the forty years of the Arian reaction that followed the Council of Nicaea, stood for and saved the Catholic faith in the Godhead of our Lord. From that long and lone confessorship *Athanasius contra mundum* has passed into a proverb; and every generation of Christians, from his own onwards, has done him honour. But before he came into prominence in the Church, and even before the Arian heresy was heard of, Athanasius had written a pair of little books; and had he done nothing else, the second of these would have entitled him to lasting fame. It is that book, the treatise *Of the Incarnation of the Word of God*, which is reproduced here. We shall best understand it if we consider the circumstances of its author's early life; and the book itself, in its turn, will illuminate his later years.

Athanasius was an Egyptian by birth and a Greek by education. His ancestors may have seen Israel go out of Egypt and the Holy Family come in; but, apart from a reference to two prophecies about that country, he shows no sign of national consciousness, nor does he, as do many of the Egyptian saints, display the Coptic temperament. His home was in Alexandria, the brilliant cosmopolitan name-city of the Macedonian conqueror who, six centuries before, had laid the foundations of Athanasius' world; and most of his life was spent in the same place. The exact date of his birth is not recorded, but it can be inferred. He was too young to remember the events of 303; and his election to the episcopate in June 328 was impugned by some on the ground that he had not reached the canonical age. It is unlikely that this was true; probably he was just thirty, and that would

17

put his birth in the first half of 298. His parents were wealthy and of good standing; and their little son, for little he always was in stature, received a liberal as well as a Christian education at the famous Catechetical School. From the circumstances of the time he received a further training, more precious than anything the fondest parent could have planned. February 303 saw the beginning of the last and greatest persecution, after forty years of peace; and this, both in its inception under Diocletian and in its recrudescence under Maximin, was particularly severe in Egypt. The Church of Alexandria, already so rich in martyrs, became richer yet; and among them were many whom Athanasius knew, men and women from whom he had learned the Catholic faith and a loving intimacy with Holy Scripture, children with whom, probably, he had worked and played. This much, and the profound impression that it made on his young soul, we know from himself in the *De Incarnatione*. The persecution ended in Egypt in 311; Athanasius from his fifth year to his fourteenth had lived in the midst of it. All through the most impressionable years of his childhood he had not only learnt the Christian faith, he had seen it in action. He had faced the possibility of martyrdom for himself; and he had made his own the faith for and by which the martyrs died—the faith of the Creator-Word Incarnate, the crucified and risen, the living and triumphant Christ.

It seems that another great influence in the life of Athanasius dates from the period of the persecution, and may have been actually a result of it. The persecutions of the third century had driven many Alexandrian Christians to take refuge in the Egyptian desert; and some had found there a life so congenial to Christian piety that, when the danger was over, they did not return. Thus was born monasticism which was destined, when persecutions were past, to take their place as the leaven of the

Church's life. The impetus to asceticism continued in the interval of peace; and thirteen years before Athanasius was born a young Copt of the name of Antony had taken up his abode as a solitary in a ruined fort at Pispir, on the right bank of the Nile. He emerged after twenty years a monument of Christian sanity; and in the Diocletian persecution, which was then beginning, he became the head and centre of monasticism in the Egyptian desert. Athanasius, who subsequently wrote Antony's life, says that he himself "was his attendant for a long time." [1] Athanasius was so early and so completely engulfed in public affairs that there seems no place for this companionship except in his boyhood; but his parents may well have sent him to the safety of the desert during the persecution, and he may have visited Antony again later. Be this as it may, it is certain that Athanasius held Antony in utmost reverence, and that there was between them, for all their difference, one of the closest and most fruitful of Christian friendships.

The persecution terminated finally with the Edict of Milan in 313; and it was about six years later that the Alexandrian presbyter Arius began to teach concerning the Word of God that "*once He was not.*" At some time before that, probably in 318, Athanasius wrote the two little books already referred to. He wrote them, so he tells us, for the instruction of one Macarius, a recent convert whom, from the affectionate friendliness of Athanasius' address, we should judge to have been a young man of about his own age. The first is entitled *Contra Gentes* or *Against the Heathen.* In this he refutes contemporary paganism and demonstrates the possibility of the knowledge of God by the human soul. In the *De Incarnatione* he sets forth the positive content of the Christian faith, as he has himself received it. Therein lies its value. It is not speculative, it is not original; as far

[1] Robertson, *op. cit.* p. 195.

19

as Christians are concerned it is not even controversial, for the need for defending the central truth of the God-head of the Word within the Church itself had not yet arisen. It is a statement of the traditional faith of the Catholic Church; and there is, in a sense, nothing of Athanasius in it, for the wonder of the mystery fills all the picture and leaves no room for the author to obtrude himself. Yet by a true Christian paradox his whole self is in it, and it is through his personality that the dynamic truth is mediated to us.

Athanasius had been a member of the Patriarch's household for some years before he wrote these books. Thereafter his rise to prominence was rapid. Though he was present at the Council of Nicaea in 325 only as a voteless deacon, he succeeded his patron in the Patri-archate of Alexandria three years later; and it was as Patriarch of Alexandria that he died, beloved and trium-phant, on May 2, 373.

The story of the intervening years has been often told, and from the external standpoint it is one of the ugliest chapters in Church History. But in Athanasius the authentic principle of redemption was at work, and he turned every circumstance to gold. Slandered, perse-cuted, exiled, the small figure moves from scene to scene, unmoved in confidence and calm. If we have read the *De Incarnatione* we know his secret. That "active, arduous peace of poise and balance in a disordered world," that steadfast, single-minded loyalty, that persevering charity, that saving humour, are the fruit of his inner absorption in the mystery of Christ. He knew that the very existence of the Church was at stake; but he was utterly certain of the truth and he knew that it must in time prevail. At the same time he was deeply conscious that the truth transcended his grasp. Forty years after the *De Incar-natione*, he wrote to his friends the monks about another book that he had tried to write, "the more I desired to write and endeavoured to force myself to understand the Divinity of the Word, so much the more did the knowledge thereof withdraw itself from me; and in proportion as I thought that I had apprehended it, in so much I perceived myself to fail of doing so. Moreover also, I was unable to express in writing even what I seemed to myself to .understand, and that which I wrote was unequal to the imperfect shadow of the truth which existed in my conception."[1]   Athanasius was not Augustine, and it needed no vision of the child by the seashore to teach him intellectual humility. The book in question has not survived, because Athanasius would not allow it to be copied. "It is not safe," he said, "that the writings of us babblers and private persons should fall into the hands of those that shall come after."[1]

His relations with the monks, the spiritual sons of Antony, run through the troubled years like a peaceful current beneath a stormy sea. The monks were unswerving in their loyalty to him; and he was consistent in his support of them. It was as "one of the ascetics" that he himself had been acclaimed for election to the episcopate; and it may be that he longed for the monastic vocation, even as Antony longed for martyrdom, and was not granted it. Even the *De Incarnatione*, written in his youth, shows the utter devotion of the monk at heart, and the same characteristic appears all through his life. When he came back to Alexandria in 338, after his first exile, old Antony left his solitude for a two days' visit to the city in order to give public testimony for the Catholic cause; and Athanasius himself escorted him on his return. Two years later, when Athanasius was again driven into exile, he took two of Antony's monks with him to Rome, where asceticism had hitherto met with small appreciation; and, by telling the Roman Christians from his own experience of Antony and "the purpose of

[1] Robertson, *op. cit.* pp. 563 f.

monks," the exiled bishop planted in the Latin Church those seeds of the monastic life which were to flower in St. Benedict and St. Bernard and the whole Religious system of the West. In 346, on his second return, he was met by greetings from Antony; and shortly afterwards he gave the seal of his approval to Pachomius' coenobitic monastery at Tabennisi by ordaining its founder as priest. The monks were Copts, and given at times to Coptic extravagance; they were for the most part uneducated, and the great Antony himself was quite illiterate. Athanasius, as we have seen, though a Copt by birth, was in all else completely Greek. But there is a wisdom of the Spirit which is independent of letters, and the monks had it. Athanasius always knew the real thing when he saw it.

Antony of the Desert, warrior and saint of God, died in 356 at the age of a hundred and five; and in the same year Athanasius was exiled for the third time. His return in 361 was short; in the following year he was exiled again until 364, and again, for the fifth time, in 365. This time, however, the end of his troubles was in sight. On February 1, 366 an order was issued for his reinstatement. The battle was won, and he had seven years of life still before him, seven years of authentic Sabbath rest, peaceful yet busy, seven years of correspondence with Basil, who was founding monasticism in Cappadocia on the Egyptian model, seven years of stabilising and consolidating his dear Egyptian Church. His passing in 373 on the second of May has somewhat obscured his fame in the Church's calendar, for, where the Divine Office is said, he loses his first Vespers to St. Philip and St. James, and his second to the Finding of the Cross. We may regret this, but Athanasius himself doubtless finds the lowest place wholly to his taste.

We will conclude with the testimony of his own contemporary, Gregory of Nazianzus, the intimate friend of

Basil. Writing a few years after Athanasius' death, he begins thus:—[1]

"In praising Athanasius I shall be praising virtue . . . because he had, or, to speak more truly, he has embraced virtue in its entirety. For all who have lived according to God's will still live unto God, though they have departed hence. . . . Again, in praising virtue I shall be praising God, Who gives virtue to men, and lifts them up . . . to Himself by the enlightenment which is akin to Himself."

To that *Non nobis, Domine*, Athanasius would be the first to say Amen. Gregory then goes on to amplify what he has said about his Christian completeness. From the study of Scripture, he says :

"He grew rich in contemplation, rich in splendour of life, combining them in wondrous sort by that golden bond which few can weave, using life as the guide of contemplation, contemplation as the seal of life."

He tells how Athanasius was raised up for the Church's need, and then describes how he fulfilled his office.

"He was sublime in action, lowly in mind; inaccessible in virtue, most accessible in intercourse; gentle, free from anger, sympathetic, sweet in words, sweeter in disposition; angelic in appearance, more angelic in mind; calm in rebuke, persuasive in praise, without spoiling the good effect of either by excess, but rebuking with the tenderness of a father, praising with the dignity of a ruler, his tenderness was not dissipated nor his severity sour, for the one was reasonable, the other prudent, and both truly wise; his disposition sufficed for the training of his spiritual children, with very little need of words; his words with very little need of the rod, and his moderate use of the rod with still less for the knife. . . . He was the patron of the wedded and of the virgin state alike, both

[1] Greg. Naz. Or. xxi., trans. Browne and Swallow, in *Nicene and Post-Nicene Fathers*, vol. vii.

peaceable and a peacemaker, and attendant upon those who are passing from hence. . . . In a good old age he closed his life, and was gathered to his fathers, the patriarchs and prophets and apostles and martyrs, who contended for the truth."

Finally, Gregory invokes Athanasius himself, the living Athanasius beyond the veil.

"O thou dear and holy one . . . mayest thou cast upon us from above a propitious glance, and conduct this people in its perfect worship of the perfect Trinity, whom as Father, Son, Holy Ghost, we contemplate and adore. And mayest thou . . . possess and aid me in my pastoral charge, uphold me, take me to thee, and set me with thyself and those like thee . . . in Christ Himself our Lord, to Whom be all glory, honour and power, for evermore. Amen."

THE INCARNATION OF THE WORD
OF GOD

CHAPTER I

CREATION AND THE FALL

§ 1

IN our former book [1] we dealt fully enough with a few of
the chief points about the heathen worship of idols, and
how those false fears originally arose. We also, by God's
grace, briefly indicated that the Word of the Father is
Himself divine, that all things that are owe their being to
His will and power, and that it is through Him that the
Father gives order to creation, by Him that all things are
moved, and through Him that they receive their being.
Now, Macarius, true lover of Christ, we must take a step
further in the faith of our holy religion, and consider also
the Word's becoming Man and His divine Appearing in
our midst. That mystery the Jews traduce, the Greeks
deride, but we adore; and your own love and devotion
to the Word also will be the greater, because in His Man-
hood He seems so little worth. For it is a fact that the
more unbelievers pour scorn on Him, so much the more
does He make His Godhead evident. The things which
they, as men, rule out as impossible, He plainly shows to
be possible; that which they deride as unfitting, His
goodness makes most fit; and things which these wiseacres laugh at as "human" He by His inherent might
declares divine. Thus by what seems His utter poverty
and weakness on the cross He overturns the pomp and
parade of idols, and quietly and hiddenly wins over the
mockers and unbelievers to recognise Him as God.

 Now in dealing with these matters it is necessary first to

[1] i.e. the *Contra Gentes*.

recall what has already been said. You must understand why it is that the Word of the Father, so great and so high, has been made manifest in bodily form. He has not assumed a body as proper to His own nature, far from it, for as the Word He is without body. He has been manifested in a human body for this reason only, out of the love and goodness of His Father, for the salvation of us men. We will begin, then, with the creation of the world and with God its Maker, for the first fact that you must grasp is this: *the renewal of creation has been wrought by the Self-same Word Who made it in the beginning.* There is thus no inconsistency between creation and salvation; for the One Father has employed the same Agent for both works, effecting the salvation of the world through the same Word Who made it in the beginning.

§ 2

In regard to the making of the universe and the creation of all things there have been various opinions, and each person has propounded the theory that suited his own taste. For instance, some say that all things are self-originated and, so to speak, haphazard. The Epicureans are among these; they deny that there is any Mind behind the universe at all. This view is contrary to all the facts of experience, their own existence included. For if all things had come into being in this automatic fashion, instead of being the outcome of Mind, though they existed, they would all be uniform and without distinction. In the universe everything would be sun or moon or whatever it was, and in the human body the whole would be hand or eye or foot. But in point of fact the sun and the moon and the earth are all different things, and even within the human body there are different members, such as foot and hand and head. This distinctness of things argues not a spontaneous generation but a prevenient

Cause; and from that Cause we can apprehend God, the Designer and Maker of all.

Others take the view expressed by Plato, that giant among the Greeks. He said that God had made all things out of pre-existent and uncreated matter, just as the carpenter makes things only out of wood that already exists. But those who hold this view do not realise that to deny that God is Himself the Cause of matter is to impute limitation to Him, just as it is undoubtedly a limitation on the part of the carpenter that he can make nothing unless he has the wood. How could God be called Maker and Artificer if His ability to make depended on some other cause, namely on matter itself? If He only worked up existing matter and did not Himself bring matter into being, He would be not the Creator but only a craftsman.

Then, again, there is the theory of the Gnostics, who have invented for themselves an Artificer of all things other than the Father of our Lord Jesus Christ. These simply shut their eyes to the obvious meaning of Scripture. For instance, the Lord, having reminded the Jews of the statement in Genesis, "He Who created them in the beginning made them male and female . . . ," and having shown that for that reason a man should leave his parents and cleave to his wife, goes on to say with reference to the Creator, "What therefore *God* has joined together, let no man put asunder."[1] How can they get a creation independent of the Father out of that? And, again, St. John, speaking all inclusively, says, "All things became by Him and without Him came nothing into being.[2] How then could the Artificer be someone different, other than the Father of Christ?

§ 3

Such are the notions which men put forward. But the impiety of their foolish talk is plainly declared by the

[1] Matt. xix. 4-6. [2] John i. 3.

divine teaching of the Christian faith. From it we know that, because there is Mind behind the universe, it did not originate itself; because God is infinite, not finite, it was not made from pre-existent matter, but out of nothing and out of non-existence absolute and utter God brought it into being through the Word. He says as much in Genesis: "In the beginning God created the heavens and the earth;[1] and again through that most helpful book *The Shepherd*, "Believe thou first and foremost that there is One God Who created and arranged all things and brought them out of non-existence into being."[2] Paul also indicates the same thing when he says, "By faith we understand that the worlds were framed by the Word of God, so that the things which we see now did not come into being out of things which had previously appeared."[3] For God is good—or rather, of all goodness He is Fountainhead, and it is impossible for one who is good to be mean or grudging about anything. Grudging existence to none therefore, He made all things out of nothing through His own Word, our Lord Jesus Christ; and of all these His earthly creatures He reserved especial mercy for the race of men. Upon them, therefore, upon men who, as animals, were essentially impermanent, He bestowed a grace which other creatures lacked—namely, the impress of His own Image, a share in the reasonable being of the very Word Himself, so that, reflecting Him and themselves becoming reasonable and expressing the Mind of God even as He does, though in limited degree, they might continue for ever in the blessed and only true life of the saints in paradise. But since the will of man could turn either way, God secured this grace that He had given by making it conditional from the first upon two things—namely, a law and a place. He set them in His own paradise, and laid upon them a single prohibition. If they guarded the grace and retained the loveliness of

[1] Gen. i. 1.   [2] *The Shepherd of Hermas*, Book II. §1.   [3] Heb. xi. 3.

their original innocence, then the life of paradise should be theirs, without sorrow, pain or care, and after it the assurance of immortality in heaven. But if they went astray and became vile, throwing away their birthright of beauty, then they would come under the natural law of death and live no longer in paradise, but, dying outside of it, continue in death and in corruption. This is what Holy Scripture tells us, proclaiming the command of God, "Of every tree that is in the garden thou shalt surely eat, but of the tree of the knowledge of good and evil ye shall not eat, but in the day that ye do eat, ye shall surely die."[1] "*Ye shall surely die*"—not just die only, but remain in the state of death and of corruption.

§ 4

You may be wondering why we are discussing the origin of men when we set out to talk about the Word's becoming Man. The former subject is relevant to the latter for this reason: it was our sorry case that caused the Word to come down, our transgression that called out His love for us, so that He made haste to help us and to appear among us. It is we who were the cause of His taking human form, and for our salvation that in His great love He was both born and manifested in a human body. For God had made man thus (that is, as an embodied spirit), and had willed that he should remain in incorruption. But men, having turned from the contemplation of God to evil of their own devising, had come inevitably under the law of death. Instead of remaining in the state in which God had created them, they were in process of becoming corrupted entirely, and death had them completely under its dominion. For the transgression of the commandment was making them turn back again according to their nature; and as they had at the

[1] Gen. ii. 16 f.

29

beginning come into being out of non-existence, so were they now on the way to returning, through corruption, to non-existence again. The presence and love of the Word had called them into being; inevitably, therefore when they lost the knowledge of God, they lost existence with it; for it is God alone Who exists, evil is non-being, the negation and antithesis of good. By nature, of course, man is mortal, since he was made from nothing; but he bears also the Likeness of Him Who is, and if he preserves that Likeness through constant contemplation, then his nature is deprived of its power and he remains incorrupt. So is it affirmed in Wisdom: "The keeping of His laws is the assurance of incorruption." [1] And being incorrupt, he would be henceforth as God, as Holy Scripture says, "I have said, Ye are gods and sons of the Highest all of you: but ye die as men and fall as one of the princes." [2]

§ 5

This, then, was the plight of men. God had not only made them out of nothing, but had also graciously bestowed on them His own life by the grace of the Word. Then, turning from eternal things to things corruptible, by counsel of the devil, they had become the cause of their own corruption in death; for, as I said before, though they were by nature subject to corruption, the grace of their union with the Word made them capable of escaping from the natural law, provided that they retained the beauty of innocence with which they were created. That is to say, the presence of the Word with them shielded them even from natural corruption, as also Wisdom says: "God created man for incorruption and as an image of His own eternity; but by envy of the devil death entered into the world." [3] When this happened, men began to die, and corruption ran riot among them and held sway

[1] Wisdom vi. 18.   [2] Psalm lxxxii. 6 f.   [3] Wisdom ii. 23 f.

over them to an even more than natural degree, because it was the penalty of which God had forewarned them for transgressing the commandment. Indeed, they had in their sinning surpassed all limits; for, having invented wickedness in the beginning and so involved themselves in death and corruption, they had gone on gradually from bad to worse, not stopping at any one kind of evil, but continually, as with insatiable appetite, devising new kinds of sins. Adulteries and thefts were everywhere, murder and rapine filled the earth, law was disregarded in corruption and injustice, all kinds of iniquities were perpetrated by all, both singly and in common. Cities were warring with cities, nations were rising against nations, and the whole earth was rent with factions and battles, while each strove to outdo the other in wickedness. Even crimes contrary to nature were not unknown, but as the martyr-apostle of Christ says: "Their women changed the natural use into that which is against nature; and the men also, leaving the natural use of the woman, flamed out in lust towards each other, perpetrating shameless acts with their own sex, and receiving in their own persons the due recompense of their pervertedness." [1]

CHAPTER II

THE DIVINE DILEMMA AND ITS SOLUTION IN THE INCARNATION

§ 6

WE saw in the last chapter that, because death and corruption were gaining ever firmer hold on them, the human race was in process of destruction. Man, who was created in God's image and in his possession of reason reflected the very Word Himself, was disappearing, and the work

[1] Rom. i. 26 f.

31

of God was being undone. The law of death, which followed from the Transgression, prevailed upon us, and from it there was no escape. The thing that was happening was in truth both monstrous and unfitting. It would, of course, have been unthinkable that God should go back upon His word and that man, having transgressed, should not die; but it was equally monstrous that beings which once had shared the nature of the Word should perish and turn back again into non-existence through corruption. It was unworthy of the goodness of God that creatures made by Him should be brought to nothing through the deceit wrought upon man by the devil; and it was supremely unfitting that the work of God in mankind should disappear, either through their own negligence or through the deceit of evil spirits. As, then, the creatures whom He had created reasonable, like the Word, were in fact perishing, and such noble works were on the road to ruin, what then was God, being Good, to do? Was He to let corruption and death have their way with them? In that case, what was the use of having made them in the beginning? Surely it would have been better never to have been created at all than, having been created, to be neglected and perish; and, besides that, such indifference to the ruin of His own work before His very eyes would argue not goodness in God but limitation, and that far more than if He had never created men at all. It was impossible, therefore, that God should leave man to be carried off by corruption, because it would be unfitting and unworthy of Himself.

§ 7

Yet, true though this is, it is not the whole matter. As we have already noted, it was unthinkable that God, the Father of Truth, should go back upon His word regarding death in order to ensure our continued existence. He could not falsify Himself; what, then, was God to do? Was He to demand repentance from men for their transgression? You might say that that was worthy of God, and argue further that, as through the Transgression they became subject to corruption, so through repentance they might return to incorruption again. But repentance would not guard the Divine consistency, for, if death did not hold dominion over men, God would still remain untrue. Nor does repentance recall men from what is according to their nature; all that it does is to make them cease from sinning. Had it been a case of a trespass only, and not of a subsequent corruption, repentance would have been well enough; but when once transgression had begun men came under the power of the corruption proper to their nature and were bereft of the grace which belonged to them as creatures in the Image of God. No, repentance could not meet the case. What—or rather *Who* was it that was needed for such grace and such recall as we required? Who, save the Word of God Himself, Who also in the beginning had made all things out of nothing? His part it was, and His alone, both to bring again the corruptible to incorruption and to maintain for the Father His consistency of character with all. For He alone, being Word of the Father and above all, was in consequence both able to recreate all, and worthy to suffer on behalf of all and to be an ambassador for all with the Father.

§ 8

For this purpose, then, the incorporeal and incorruptible and immaterial Word of God entered our world. In one sense, indeed, He was not far from it before, for no part of creation had ever been without Him Who, while ever abiding in union with the Father, yet fills all things that are. But now He entered the world in a new way, stooping to our level in His love and Self-revealing to us. He saw the reasonable race, the race of men that, like Himself, expressed the Father's Mind, wasting out of

33

existence, and death reigning over all in corruption. He saw that corruption held us all the closer, because it was the penalty for the Transgression; He saw, too, how unthinkable it would be for the law to be repealed before it was fulfilled. He saw how unseemly it was that the very things of which He Himself was the Artificer should be disappearing. He saw how the surpassing wickedness of men was mounting up against them; He saw also their universal liability to death. All this He saw and, pitying our race, moved with compassion for our limitation, unable to endure that death should have the mastery, rather than that His creatures should perish and the work of His Father for us men come to nought, He took to Himself a body, a human body even as our own. Nor did He will merely to become embodied or merely to appear; had that been so, He could have revealed His divine majesty in some other and better way. No, He took *our* body, and not only so, but He took it directly from a spotless, stainless virgin, without the agency of human father—a pure body, untainted by intercourse with man. He, the Mighty One, the Artificer of all, Himself prepared this body in the virgin as a temple for Himself, and took it for His very own, as the instrument through which He was known and in which He dwelt. Thus, taking a body like our own, because all our bodies were liable to the corruption of death, He surrendered His body to death in place of all, and offered it to the Father. This He did out of sheer love for us, so that in His death all might die, and the law of death thereby be abolished because, when He had fulfilled in His body that for which it was appointed, it was thereafter voided of its power for men. This He did that He might turn again to incorruption men who had turned back to corruption, and make them alive through death by the appropriation of His body and by the grace of His resurrection. Thus He would make death to disappear from them as utterly as straw from fire. 34

The Word perceived that corruption could not be got rid of otherwise than through death; yet He Himself, as the Word, being immortal and the Father's Son, was such as could not die. For this reason, therefore, He assumed a body capable of death, in order that it, through belonging to the Word Who is above all, might become in dying a sufficient exchange for all, and, itself remaining incorruptible through His indwelling, might thereafter put an end to corruption for all others as well, by the grace of the resurrection. It was by surrendering to death the body which He had taken, as an offering and sacrifice free from every stain, that He forthwith abolished death for His human brethren by the offering of the equivalent. For naturally, since the Word of God was above all, when He offered His own temple and bodily instrument as a substitute for the life of all, He fulfilled in death all that was required. Naturally also, through this union of the immortal Son of God with our human nature, all men were clothed with incorruption in the promise of the resurrection. For the solidarity of mankind is such that, by virtue of the Word's indwelling in a single human body, the corruption which goes with death has lost its power over all. You know how it is when some great king enters a large city and dwells in one of its houses; because of his dwelling in that single house, the whole city is honoured, and enemies and robbers cease to molest it. Even so is it with the King of all; He has come into our country and dwelt in one body amidst the many, and in consequence the designs of the enemy against mankind have been foiled, and the corruption of death, which formerly held them in its power, has simply ceased to be. For the human race would have perished utterly had not the Lord and Saviour of all, the Son of God, come among us to put an end to death.

This great work was, indeed, supremely worthy of the goodness of God. A king who has founded a city, so far from neglecting it when through the carelessness of the inhabitants it is attacked by robbers, avenges it and saves it from destruction, having regard rather to his own honour than to the people's neglect. Much more, then, the Word of the All-good Father was not unmindful of the human race that He had called to be; but rather, by the offering of His own body He abolished the death which they had incurred, and corrected their neglect by His own teaching. Thus by His own power He restored the whole nature of man. The Saviour's own inspired disciples assure us of this. We read in one place: "For the love of Christ constraineth us, because we thus judge that, if One died on behalf of all, then all died, and He died for all that we should no longer live unto ourselves, but unto Him who died and rose again from the dead, even our Lord Jesus Christ." [1] And again another says: "But we behold Him Who hath been made a little lower than the angels, even Jesus, because of the suffering of death crowned with glory and honour, that by the grace of God He should taste of death on behalf of every man." The same writer goes on to point out why it was necessary for God the Word and none other to become Man: "For it became Him, for Whom are all things and through Whom are all things, in bringing many sons unto glory, to make the Author of their salvation perfect through suffering." [2] He means that the rescue of mankind from corruption was the proper part only of Him Who made them in the beginning. He points out also that the Word assumed a human body, expressly in order that He might offer it in sacrifice for other like bodies: "Since then the children

[1] 2 Cor. v. 14 f.   [2] Heb. ii. 9 ff.

are sharers in flesh and blood, He also Himself assumed the same, in order that through death He might bring to nought Him that hath the power of death, that is to say, the Devil, and might rescue those who all their lives were enslaved by the fear of death." [1] For by the sacrifice of His own body He did two things: He put an end to the law of death which barred our way; and He made a new beginning of life for us, by giving us the hope of resurrection. By man death has gained its power over men; by the Word made Man death has been destroyed and life raised up anew. That is what Paul says, that true servant of Christ: "For since by man came death, by man came also the resurrection of the dead. Just as in Adam all die, even so in Christ shall all be made alive," [2] and so forth. Now, therefore, when we die we no longer do so as men condemned to death, but as those who are even now in process of rising we await the general resurrection of all, "which in its own times He shall show," [3] even God Who wrought it and bestowed it on us.

This, then, is the first cause of the Saviour's becoming Man. There are, however, other things which show how wholly fitting is His blessed presence in our midst; and these we must now go on to consider.

CHAPTER III

THE DIVINE DILEMMA AND ITS SOLUTION IN THE INCARNATION—*continued*

§ 11

WHEN God the Almighty was making mankind through His own Word, He perceived that they, owing to the

[1] Heb. ii. 14 f. [2] 1 Cor. xv. 21 f. [3] 1 Tim. vi. 15.

limitation of their nature, could not of themselves have any knowledge of their Artificer, the Incorporeal and Uncreate. He took pity on them, therefore, and did not leave them destitute of the knowledge of Himself, lest their very existence should prove purposeless. For of what use is existence to the creature if it cannot know its Maker? How could men be reasonable beings if they had no knowledge of the Word and Reason of the Father, through Whom they had received their being? They would be no better than the beasts, had they no knowledge save of earthly things; and why should God have made them at all, if He had not intended them to know Him? But, in fact, the good God has given them a share in His own Image, that is, in our Lord Jesus Christ, and has made even themselves after the same Image and Likeness. Why? Simply in order that through this gift of God-likeness in themselves they may be able to perceive the Image Absolute, that is the Word Himself, and through Him to apprehend the Father; which knowledge of their Maker is for men the only really happy and blessed life.

But, as we have already seen, men, foolish as they are, thought little of the grace they had received, and turned away from God. They defiled their own soul so completely that they not only lost their apprehension of God, but invented for themselves other gods of various kinds. They fashioned idols for themselves in place of the truth and reverenced things that are not, rather than God Who is, as St. Paul says, "worshipping the creature rather than the Creator." [1] Moreover, and much worse, they transferred the honour which is due to God to material objects such as wood and stone, and also to man; and further even than that they went, as we said in our former book. Indeed, so impious were they that they worshipped evil spirits as gods in satisfaction of their lusts. They sacrificed brute beasts and immolated men, as the just due of these

[1] Rom. i. 25.

38

deities, thereby bringing themselves more and more under their insane control. Magic arts also were taught among them, oracles in sundry places led men astray, and the cause of everything in human life was traced to the stars, as though nothing existed but that which could be seen. In a word, impiety and lawlessness were everywhere, and neither God nor His Word was known. Yet He had not hidden Himself from the sight of men nor given the knowledge of Himself in one way only; but rather He had unfolded it in many forms and by many ways.

§ 12

God knew the limitation of mankind, you see; and though the grace of being made in His Image was sufficient to give them knowledge of the Word and through Him of the Father, as a safeguard against their neglect of this grace, He provided the works of creation also as means by which the Maker might be known. Nor was this all. Man's neglect of the indwelling grace tends ever to increase; and against this further frailty also God made provision by giving them a law, and by sending prophets, men whom they knew. Thus, if they were tardy in looking up to heaven, they might still gain knowledge of their Maker from those close at hand; for men can learn directly about higher things from other men. Three ways thus lay open to them, by which they might obtain the knowledge of God. They could look up into the immensity of heaven, and by pondering the harmony of creation come to know its Ruler, the Word of the Father, Whose all-ruling providence makes known the Father to all. Or, if this was beyond them, they could converse with holy men, and through them learn to know God, the Artificer of all things, the Father of Christ, and to recognise the worship of idols as the negation of the truth and full of all impiety. Or else, in the third place, they could cease from lukewarmness and lead a good life merely by knowing the law. For the law was not given only for the Jews, nor was it solely for their sake that God sent the prophets, though it was to the Jews that they were sent and by the Jews that they were persecuted. The law and the prophets were a sacred school of the knowledge of God and the conduct of the spiritual life for the whole world.

So great, indeed, were the goodness and the love of God. Yet men, bowed down by the pleasures of the moment and by the frauds and illusions of the evil spirits, did not lift up their heads towards the truth. So burdened were they with their wickednesses that they seemed rather to be brute beasts than reasonable men, reflecting the very Likeness of the Word.

§ 13

What was God to do in face of this dehumanising of mankind, this universal hiding of the knowledge of Himself by the wiles of evil spirits? Was He to keep silence before so great a wrong and let men go on being thus deceived and kept in ignorance of Himself? If so, what was the use of having made them in His own Image originally? It would surely have been better for them always to have been brutes, rather than to revert to that condition when once they had shared the nature of the Word. Again, things being as they were, what was the use of their ever having had the knowledge of God? Surely it would have been better for God never to have bestowed it, than that men should subsequently be found unworthy to receive it. Similarly, what possible profit could it be to God Himself, Who made men, if when made they did not worship Him, but regarded others as their makers? This would be tantamount to His having made them for others and not for Himself. Even an earthly king, though he is only a man, does not allow lands that he has colonised to pass into other hands or to desert to other rulers, but sends letters and friends and even visits them himself to recall them to their allegiance, rather than allow His work to be undone. How much more, then, will God be patient and painstaking with His creatures, that they be not led astray from Him to the service of those that are not, and that all the more because such error means for them sheer ruin, and because it is not right that those who had once shared His Image should be destroyed.

What, then, was God to do? What else could He possibly do, being God, but renew His Image in mankind, so that through it men might once more come to know Him? And how could this be done save by the coming of the very Image Himself, our Saviour Jesus Christ? Men could not have done it, for they are only made after the Image; nor could angels have done it, for they are not the images of God. The Word of God came in His own Person, because it was He alone, the Image of the Father, Who could recreate man made after the Image.

In order to effect this re-creation, however, He had first to do away with death and corruption. Therefore He assumed a human body, in order that in it death might once for all be destroyed, and that men might be renewed according to the Image. The Image of the Father only was sufficient for this need. Here is an illustration to prove it.

§ 14

You know what happens when a portrait that has been painted on a panel becomes obliterated through external stains. The artist does not throw away the panel, but the subject of the portrait has to come and sit for it again, and then the likeness is re-drawn on the same material. Even

41

so was it with the All-holy Son of God. He, the Image of the Father, came and dwelt in our midst, in order that He might renew mankind made after Himself, and seek out His lost sheep, even as He says in the Gospel: "I came to seek and to save that which was lost." [1] This also explains His saying to the Jews: "Except a man be born anew . . ." [2] He was not referring to a man's natural birth from his mother, as they thought, but to the re-birth and re-creation of the soul in the Image of God.

Nor was this the only thing which only the Word could do. When the madness of idolatry and irreligion filled the world and the knowledge of God was hidden, whose part was it to teach the world about the Father? Man's, would you say? But men cannot run everywhere over the world, nor would their words carry sufficient weight if they did, nor would they be, unaided, a match for the evil spirits. Moreover, since even the best of men were confused and blinded by evil, how could they convert the souls and minds of others? You cannot put straight in others what is warped in yourself. Perhaps you will say, then, that creation was enough to teach men about the Father. But if that had been so, such great evils would never have occurred. Creation was there all the time, but it did not prevent men from wallowing in error. Once more, then, it was the Word of God, Who sees all that is in man and moves all things in creation, Who alone could meet the needs of the situation. It was His part and His alone, Whose ordering of the universe reveals the Father, to renew the same teaching. But how was He to do it? By the same means as before, perhaps you will say, that is, through the works of creation. But this was proven insufficient. Men had neglected to consider the heavens before, and now they were looking in the opposite direction. Wherefore, in all naturalness and fitness, desiring to do good to men, as Man He dwells, taking to Himself

[1] Luke xix. 10.   [2] John iii. 3.

42

a body like the rest; and through His actions done in that body, as it were on their own level, He teaches those who would not learn by other means to know Himself, the Word of God, and through Him the Father.

§ 15

He deals with them as a good teacher with his pupils, coming down to their level and using simple means. St. Paul says as much: "Because in the wisdom of God the world in its wisdom knew not God, God thought fit through the simplicity of the News proclaimed to save those who believe." [1] Men had turned from the contemplation of God above, and were looking for Him in the opposite direction, down among created things and things of sense. The Saviour of us all, the Word of God, in His great love took to Himself a body and moved as Man among men, meeting their senses, so to speak, half way. He became Himself an object for the senses, so that those who were seeking God in sensible things might apprehend the Father through the works which He, the Word of God, did in the body. Human and human-minded as men were, therefore, to whichever side they looked in the sensible world they found themselves taught the truth. Were they awe-stricken by creation? They beheld it confessing Christ as Lord. Did their minds tend to regard men as Gods? The uniqueness of the Saviour's works marked Him, alone of men, as Son of God. Were they drawn to evil spirits? They saw them driven out by the Lord and learned that the Word of God alone was God and that the evil spirits were not gods at all. Were they inclined to hero-worship and the cult of the dead? Then the fact that the Saviour had risen from the dead showed them how false these other deities were, and that the Word of the Father is the one true

[1] i Cor. i. 21.

43

Lord, the Lord even of death. For this reason was He both born and manifested as Man, for this He died and rose, in order that, eclipsing by His works all other human deeds, He might recall men from all the paths of error to know the Father. As He says Himself, "I came to seek and to save that which was lost." [1]

§ 16

When, then, the minds of men had fallen finally to the level of sensible things, the Word submitted to appear in a body, in order that He, as Man, might centre their senses on Himself, and convince them through His human acts that He Himself is not man only but also God, the Word and Wisdom of the true God. This is what Paul wants to tell us when he says: "That ye, being rooted and grounded in love, may be strong to apprehend with all the saints what is the length and breadth and height and depth, and to know the love of God that surpasses knowledge, so that ye may be filled unto all the fulness of God." [2] The Self-revealing of the Word is in every dimension—above, in creation; below, in the Incarnation; in the depth, in Hades; in the breadth, throughout the world. All things have been filled with the knowledge of God.

For this reason He did not offer the sacrifice on behalf of all immediately He came, for if He had surrendered His body to death and then raised it again at once He would have ceased to be an object of our senses. Instead of that, He stayed in His body and let Himself be seen in it, doing acts and giving signs which showed Him to be not only man, but also God the Word. There were thus two things which the Saviour did for us by becoming Man. He banished death from us and made us anew; and, invisible and imperceptible as in Himself He is, He became

[1] Luke xix. 10.   [2] Eph. iii. 17 ff.

44

visible through His works and revealed Himself as the Word of the Father, the Ruler and King of the whole creation.

There is a paradox in this last statement which we must now examine. The Word was not hedged in by His body, nor did His presence in the body prevent His being present elsewhere as well. When He moved His body He did not cease also to direct the universe by His Mind and might. No. The marvellous truth is, that being the Word, so far from being Himself contained by anything, He actually contained all things Himself. In creation He is present everywhere, yet is distinct in being from it; ordering, directing, giving life to all, containing all, yet is He Himself the Uncontained, existing solely in His Father. As with the whole, so also is it with the part. Existing in a human body, to which He Himself gives life, He is still Source of life to all the universe, present in every part of it, yet outside the whole; and He is revealed both through the works of His body and through His activity in the world. It is, indeed, the function of soul to *behold* things that are outside the body, but it cannot energise or move them. A man cannot transport things from one place to another, for instance, merely by thinking about them; nor can you or I move the sun and the stars just by sitting at home and looking at them. With the Word of God in His human nature, however, it was otherwise. His body was for Him not a limitation, but an instrument, so that He was both in it and in all things, and outside all things, resting in the Father alone. At one and the same time—this is the wonder—as Man He was living a human life, and as Word He was sustaining the life of the universe, and as Son He was in constant union with the Father. Not even His birth from a virgin,

45

therefore, changed Him in any way, nor was He defiled by being in the body. Rather, He sanctified the body by being in it. For His being in everything does not mean that He shares the nature of everything, only that He gives all things their being and sustains them in it. Just as the sun is not defiled by the contact of its rays with earthly objects, but rather enlightens and purifies them, so He Who made the sun is not defiled by being made known in a body, but rather the body is cleansed and quickened by His indwelling, "Who did no sin, neither was guile found in His mouth." [1]

§ 18

You must understand, therefore, that when writers on this sacred theme speak of Him as eating and drinking and being born, they mean that the body, as a body, was born and sustained with the food proper to its nature; while God the Word, Who was united with it, was at the same time ordering the universe and revealing Himself through His bodily acts as not man only but God. Those acts are rightly said to be His acts, because the body which did them did indeed belong to Him and none other; moreover, it was right that they should be thus attributed to Him as Man, in order to show that His body was a real one and not merely an appearance. From such ordinary acts as being born and taking food, He was recognised as being actually present in the body; but by the extraordinary acts which He did through the body He proved Himself to be the Son of God. That is the meaning of His words to the unbelieving Jews: "If I do not the works of My Father, believe Me not; but if I do, even if ye believe not Me, believe My works, that ye may know that the Father is in Me and I in the Father."

Invisible in Himself, He is known from the works of

[1] 1 Peter ii. 22.

creation; so also, when His Godhead is veiled in human nature, His bodily acts still declare Him to be not man only, but the Power and Word of God. To speak authoritatively to evil spirits, for instance, and to drive them out, is not human but divine; and who could see-Him curing all the diseases to which mankind is prone, and still deem Him mere man and not also God? He cleansed lepers, He made the lame to walk, He opened the ears of the deaf and the eyes of the blind, there was no sickness or weakness that He did not drive away. Even the most casual observer can see that these were acts of God. The healing of the man born blind, for instance, who but the Father and Artificer of man, the Controller of his whole being, could thus have restored the faculty denied at birth? He Who did thus must surely be Himself the Lord of birth. This is proved also at the outset of His becoming Man. He formed His own body from the virgin; and that is no small proof of His Godhead, since He Who made that was the Maker of all else. And would not anyone infer from the fact of that body being begotten of a virgin only, without human father, that He Who appeared in it was also the Maker and Lord of all beside?

Again, consider the miracle at Cana. Would not anyone who saw the substance of water transmuted into wine understand that He Who did it was the Lord and Maker of the water that He changed? It was for the same reason that He walked on the sea as on dry land—to prove to the onlookers that He had mastery over all. And the feeding of the multitude, when He made little into much, so that from five loaves five thousand mouths were filled--did not that prove Him none other than the very Lord Whose Mind is over all?

CHAPTER IV

THE DEATH OF CHRIST

§ 19

ALL these things the Saviour thought fit to do, so that, recognising His bodily acts as works of God, men who were blind to His presence in creation might regain knowledge of the Father. For, as I said before, who that saw His authority over evil spirits and their response to it could doubt that He was, indeed, the Son, the Wisdom and the Power of God? Even the very creation broke silence at His behest and, marvellous to relate, confessed with one voice before the cross, that monument of victory, that He Who suffered thereon in the body was not man only, but Son of God and Saviour of all. The sun veiled his face, the earth quaked, the mountains were rent asunder, all men were stricken with awe. These things showed that Christ on the cross was God, and that all creation was His slave and was bearing witness by its fear to the presence of its Master.

Thus, then, God the Word revealed Himself to men through His works. We must next consider the end of His earthly life and the nature of His bodily death. This is, indeed, the very centre of our faith, and everywhere you hear men speak of it; by it, too, no less than by His other acts, Christ is revealed as God and Son of God.

§ 20

We have dealt as far as circumstances and our own understanding permit with the reason for His bodily manifestation. We have seen that to change the corruptible to incorruption was proper to none other than the Saviour Himself, Who in the beginning made all things out of nothing; that only the Image of the Father could re-create the likeness of the Image in men, that none save our Lord Jesus Christ could give to mortals immortality, and that only the Word Who orders all things and is alone the Father's true and sole-begotten Son could teach men about Him and abolish the worship of idols. But beyond all this, there was a debt owing which must needs be paid; for, as I said before, all men were due to die. Here, then, is the second reason why the Word dwelt among us, namely that having proved His Godhead by His works, He might offer the sacrifice on behalf of all, surrendering His own temple to death in place of all, to settle man's account with death and free him from the primal transgression. In the same act also He showed Himself mightier than death, displaying His own body incorruptible as the first-fruits of the resurrection.

You must not be surprised if we repeat ourselves in dealing with this subject. We are speaking of the good pleasure of God and of the things which He in His loving wisdom thought fit to do, and it is better to put the same thing in several ways than to run the risk of leaving something out. The body of the Word, then, being a real human body, in spite of its having been uniquely formed from a virgin, was of itself mortal and, like other bodies, liable to death. But the indwelling of the Word loosed it from this natural liability, so that corruption could not touch it. Thus it happened that two opposite marvels took place at once : the death of all was consummated in the Lord's body ; yet, because the Word was in it, death and corruption were in the same act utterly abolished. Death there had to be, and death for all, so that the due of all might be paid. Wherefore, the Word, as I said, being Himself incapable of death, assumed a mortal body, that He might offer it as His own in place of all, and suffering for the sake of all through His union with it, "might bring to nought Him that had the power of death, that is, the devil, and might deliver them who all their lifetime were enslaved by the fear of death." [1]

[1] Heb. ii. 14 f.

49

Have no fear, then. Now that the common Saviour of all has died on our behalf, we who believe in Christ no longer die, as men died aforetime, in fulfilment of the threat of the law. That condemnation has come to an end; and now that, by the grace of the resurrection, corruption has been banished and done away, we are loosed from our mortal bodies in God's good time for each, so that we may obtain thereby a better resurrection. Like seeds cast into the earth, we do not perish in our dissolution, but like them shall rise again, death having been brought to nought by the grace of the Saviour. That is why blessed Paul, through whom we all have surety of the resurrection, says: "This corruptible must put on incorruption and this mortal must put on immortality; but when this corruptible shall have put on incorruption and this mortal shall have put on immortality, then shall be brought to pass the saying that is written, 'Death is swallowed up in victory. O Death, where is thy sting? O Grave, where is thy victory?'" [1]

"Well then," some people may say, "if the essential thing was that He should surrender His body to death in place of all, why did He not do so as Man privately, without going to the length of public crucifixion? Surely it would have been more suitable for Him to have laid aside His body with honour than to endure so shameful a death." But look at this argument closely, and see how merely human it is, whereas what the Saviour did was truly divine and worthy of His Godhead for several reasons. The first is this. The death of men under ordinary circumstances is the result of their natural weakness. They are essentially impermanent, so after a time they fall ill and when worn out they die. But the

[1] I Cor. xv. 53 ff.

Lord is not like that. He is not weak, He is the Power of God and Word of God and Very Life Itself. If He had died quietly in His bed like other men it would have looked as if He did so in accordance with His nature, and as though He was indeed no more than other men. But because He was Himself Word and Life and Power His body was made strong, and because the death had to be accomplished, He took the occasion of perfecting His sacrifice not from Himself, but from others. How could He fall sick, Who had healed others? Or how could that body weaken and fail by means of which others are made strong? Here, again, you may say, "Why did He not prevent death, as He did sickness?" Because it was precisely in order to be able to die that He had taken a body, and to prevent the death would have been to impede the resurrection. And as to the unsuitability of sickness for His body, as arguing weakness, you may say, "Did He then not hunger?" Yes, He hungered, because that was the property of His body, but He did not die of hunger, because He Whose body hungered was the Lord. Similarly, though He died to ransom all, He did not see corruption. His body rose in perfect soundness, for it was the body of none other than the Life Himself.

§ 22

Someone else might say, perhaps, that it would have been better for the Lord to have avoided the designs of the Jews against Him, and so to have guarded His body from death altogether. But see how unfitting this also would have been for Him. Just as it would not have been fitting for Him to give His body to death by His own hand, being Word and being Life, so also it was not consonant with Himself that He should avoid the death inflicted by others. Rather, He pursued it to the uttermost, and in pursuance of His nature neither laid aside His body of

His own accord nor escaped the plotting Jews. And this action showed no limitation or weakness in the Word; for He both waited for death in order to make an end of it, and hastened to accomplish it as an offering on behalf of all. Moreover, as it was the death of all mankind that the Saviour came to accomplish, not His own, He did not lay aside His body by an individual act of dying, for to Him, as Life, this simply did not belong; but He accepted death at the hands of men, thereby completely to destroy it in His own body.

There are some further considerations which enable one to understand why the Lord's body had such an end. The supreme object of His coming was to bring about the resurrection of the body. This was to be the monument to His victory over death, the assurance to all that He had Himself conquered corruption and that their own bodies also would eventually be incorrupt; and it was in token of that and as a pledge of the future resurrection that He kept His body incorrupt. But there again, if His body had fallen sick and the Word had left it in that condition, how unfitting it would have been! Should He Who healed the bodies of others neglect to keep His own in health? How would His miracles of healing be believed, if this were so? Surely people would either laugh at Him as unable to dispel disease or else consider Him lacking in proper human feeling because He could do so, but did not.

§ 23

Then, again, suppose without any illness He had just concealed His body somewhere, and then suddenly reappeared and said that He had risen from the dead. He would have been regarded merely as a teller of tales, and because there was no witness of His death, nobody would believe His resurrection. Death had to precede resurrection, for there could be no resurrection without it. A secret and unwitnessed death would have left the resurrection without any proof or evidence to support it. Again, why should He die a secret death, when He proclaimed the fact of His rising openly? Why should He drive out evil spirits and heal the man blind from birth and change water into wine, all publicly, in order to convince men that He was the Word, and not also declare publicly that incorruptibility of His mortal body, so that He might Himself be believed to be the Life? And how could His disciples have had boldness in speaking of the resurrection unless they could state it as a fact that He had first died? Or how could their hearers be expected to believe their assertion, unless they themselves also had witnessed His death? For if the Pharisees at the time refused to believe and forced others to deny also, though the things had happened before their very eyes, how many excuses for unbelief would they have contrived, if it had taken place secretly? Or how could the end of death and the victory over it have been declared, had not the Lord thus challenged it before the sight of all, and by the incorruption of His body proved that henceforward it was annulled and void?

§ 24

There are some other possible objections that must be answered. Some might urge that, even granting the necessity of a public death for subsequent belief in the resurrection, it would surely have been better for Him to have arranged an honourable death for Himself, and so to have avoided the ignominy of the cross. But even this would have given ground for suspicion that His power over death was limited to the particular kind of death which He chose for Himself; and that again would furnish excuse for disbelieving the resurrection. Death came to His body, therefore, not from Himself but from enemy action, in order that the Saviour might utterly abolish death in whatever form they offered it to Him. A generous wrestler, virile and strong, does not himself choose his antagonists, lest it should be thought that of some of them he is afraid. Rather, he lets the spectators choose them, and that all the more if these are hostile, so that he may overthrow whomsoever they match against him and thus vindicate his superior strength. Even so was it with Christ. He, the Life of all, our Lord and Saviour, did not arrange the manner of his own death lest He should seem to be afraid of some other kind. No. He accepted and bore upon the cross a death inflicted by others, and those others His special enemies, a death which to them was supremely terrible and by no means to be faced; and He did this in order that, by destroying even this death, He might Himself be believed to be the Life, and the power of death be recognised as finally annulled. A marvellous and mighty paradox has thus occurred, for the death which they thought to inflict on Him as dishonour and disgrace has become the glorious monument to death's defeat. Therefore it is also, that He neither endured the death of John, who was beheaded, nor was He sawn asunder, like Isaiah: even in death He preserved His body whole and undivided, so that there should be no excuse hereafter for those who would divide the Church.

§ 25

So much for the objections of those outside the Church. But if any honest Christian wants to know why He suffered death on the cross and not in some other way, we answer thus: in no other way was it expedient for us, indeed the Lord offered for our sakes the one death that was supremely good. He had come to bear the curse that lay on us; and how could He "become a curse" [1] otherwise than

[1] Gal. iii. 13.

by accepting the accursed death? And that death is the cross, for it is written "Cursed is every one that hangeth on a tree." [1] Again, the death of the Lord is the ransom of all, and by it "the middle wall of partition" [2] is broken down and the call of the Gentiles comes about. How could He have called us if He had not been crucified, for it is only on the cross that a man dies with arms outstretched? Here, again, we see the fitness of His death and of those outstretched arms: it was that He might draw His ancient people with the one and the Gentiles with the other, and join both together in Himself. Even so, He foretold the manner of His redeeming death, "I, if I be lifted up, will draw all men unto Myself." [3] Again, the air is the sphere of the devil, the enemy of our race who, having fallen from heaven, endeavours with the other evil spirits who shared in his disobedience both to keep souls from the truth and to hinder the progress of those who are trying to follow it. The apostle refers to this when he says, "According to the prince of the power of the air, of the spirit that now worketh in the sons of disobedience." [4] But the Lord came to overthrow the devil and to purify the air and to make "a way" for us up to heaven, as the apostle says, "through the veil, that is to say, His flesh." [5] This had to be done through death, and by what other kind of death could it be done, save by a death in the air, that is, on the cross? Here, again, you see how right and natural it was that the Lord should suffer thus; for being thus "lifted up," He cleansed the air from all the evil influences of the enemy. "I beheld Satan as lightning falling," [6] He says; and thus He re-opened the road to heaven, saying again, "Lift up your gates, O ye princes, and be ye lift up, ye everlasting doors." [7] For it was not the Word Himself Who needed an opening of the gates, He being Lord of all, nor was any of His works closed to their Maker. No,

[1] Gal. iii. 13.   [2] Eph. ii. 14.   [3] John xii. 32.   [4] Eph. ii. 2.
[5] Heb. x. 20.   [6] Luke x. 18.   [7] Psalm xxiv. 7.

it was we who needed it, we whom He Himself upbore in His own body—that body which He first offered to death on behalf of all, and then made through it a path to heaven.

CHAPTER V

THE RESURRECTION

§ 26

FITTING indeed, then, and wholly consonant was the death on the cross for us; and we can see how reasonable it was, and why it is that the salvation of the world could be accomplished in no other way. Even on the cross He did not hide Himself from sight; rather, He made all creation witness to the presence of its Maker. Then, having once let it be seen that it was truly dead, He did not allow that temple of His body to linger long, but forthwith on the third day raised it up, impassible and incorruptible, the pledge and token of His victory.

It was, of course, within His power thus to have raised His body and displayed it as alive directly after death. But the all-wise Saviour did not do this, lest some should deny that it had really or completely died. Besides this, had the interval between His death and resurrection been but two days, the glory of His incorruption might not have appeared. He waited one whole day to show that His body was really dead, and then on the third day showed it incorruptible to all. The interval was no longer, lest people should have forgotten about it and grown doubtful whether it were in truth the same body. No, while the affair was still ringing in their ears and their eyes were still straining and their minds in turmoil, and while those who had put Him to death were still on the spot and themselves witnessing to the fact of it, the Son of God after three days showed His once dead body immortal and incorruptible; and it was evident to all that it was from no natural weakness that the body which the Word indwelt had died, but in order that in it by the Saviour's power death might be done away.

§ 27

A very strong proof of this destruction of death and its conquest by the cross is supplied by a present fact, namely this. All the disciples of Christ despise death; they take the offensive against it and, instead of fearing it, by the sign of the cross and by faith in Christ trample on it as on something dead. Before the divine sojourn of the Saviour, even the holiest of men were afraid of death, and mourned the dead as those who perish. But now that the Saviour has raised His body, death is no longer terrible, but all those who believe in Christ tread it underfoot as nothing, and prefer to die rather than to deny their faith in Christ, knowing full well that when they die they do not perish, but live indeed, and become incorruptible through the resurrection. But that devil who of old wickedly exulted in death, now that the pains of death are loosed, he alone it is who remains truly dead. There is proof of this too; for men who, before they believe in Christ, think death horrible and are afraid of it, once they are converted despise it so completely that they go eagerly to meet it, and themselves become witnesses of the Saviour's resurrection from it. Even children hasten thus to die, and not men only, but women train themselves by bodily discipline to meet it. So weak has death become that even women, who used to be taken in by it, mock at it now as a dead thing robbed of all its strength. Death has become like a tyrant who has been completely conquered by the legitimate monarch; bound hand and foot **as he now is,** the passers-by jeer at him, hitting him and abusing him, no longer afraid of his cruelty and rage, because of the king who has conquered him. So has death been conquered and branded for what it is by the Saviour on the cross. It is bound hand and foot, all who are in Christ trample it as they pass and as witnesses to Him deride it, scoffing and saying, "O Death, where is thy victory? O Grave, where is thy sting?"[1]

§ 28

Is this a slender proof of the impotence of death, do you think? Or is it a slight indication of the Saviour's victory over it, when boys and young girls who are in Christ look beyond this present life and train themselves to die? Every one is by nature afraid of death and of bodily dissolution; the marvel of marvels is that he who is enfolded in the faith of the cross despises this natural fear and for the sake of the cross is no longer cowardly in face of it. The natural property of fire is to burn. Suppose, then, that there was a substance such as the Indian asbestos is said to be, which had no fear of being burnt, but rather displayed the impotence of the fire by proving itself unburnable. If anyone doubted the truth of this, all he need do would be to wrap himself up in the substance in question and then touch the fire. Or, again, to revert to our former figure, if anyone wanted to see the tyrant bound and helpless, who used to be such a terror to others, he could do so simply by going into the country of the tyrant's conqueror. Even so, if anyone still doubts the conquest of death, after so many proofs and so many martyrdoms in Christ and such daily scorn of death by His truest servants, he certainly does well to marvel at so great a thing, but he must not be obstinate in unbelief and disregard of plain facts. No, he must be like the man who wants to prove the property of the asbestos, and like

[1] I Cor. xv. 55.

him who enters the conqueror's dominions to see the tyrant bound. He must embrace the faith of Christ, this disbeliever in the conquest of death, and come to His teaching. Then he will see how impotent death is and how completely conquered. Indeed, there have been many former unbelievers and deriders who, after they became believers, so scorned death as even themselves to become martyrs for Christ's sake.

§ 29

If, then, it is by the sign of the cross and by faith in Christ that death is trampled underfoot, it is clear that it is Christ Himself and none other Who is the Arch-victor over death and has robbed it of its power. Death used to be strong and terrible, but now, since the sojourn of the Saviour and the death and resurrection of His body, it is despised; and obviously it is by the very Christ Who mounted on the cross that it has been destroyed and vanquished finally. When the sun rises after the night and the whole world is lit up by it, nobody doubts that it is the sun which has thus shed its light everywhere and driven away the dark. Equally clear is it, since this utter scorning and trampling down of death has ensued upon the Saviour's manifestation in the body and His death on the cross, that it is He Himself Who brought death to nought and daily raises monuments to His victory in His own disciples. How can you think otherwise, when you see men naturally weak hastening to death, unafraid at the prospect of corruption, fearless of the descent into Hades, even indeed with eager soul provoking it, not shrinking from tortures, but preferring thus to rush on death for Christ's sake, rather than to remain in this present life? If you see with your own eyes men and women and children, even, thus welcoming death for the sake of Christ's religion, how can you be so utterly silly and incredulous and maimed in

59

your mind as not to realise that Christ, to Whom these all bear witness, Himself gives the victory to each, making death completely powerless for those who hold His faith and bear the sign of the cross? No one in his senses doubts that a snake is dead when he sees it trampled underfoot, especially when he knows how savage it used to be; nor, if he sees boys making fun of a lion, does he doubt that the brute is either dead or completely bereft of strength. These things can be seen with our own eyes, and it is the same with the conquest of death. Doubt no longer, then, when you see death mocked and scorned by those who believe in Christ, that by Christ death was destroyed, and the corruption that goes with it resolved and brought to end.

§ 30

What we have said is, indeed, no small proof of the destruction of death and of the fact that the cross of the Lord is the monument to His victory. But the resurrection of the body to immortality, which results henceforward from the work of Christ, the common Saviour and true Life of all, is more effectively proved by facts than by words to those whose mental vision is sound. For, if, as we have shown, death was destroyed and everybody tramples on it because of Christ, how much more did He Himself first trample and destroy it in His own body! Death having been slain by Him, then, what other issue could there be than the resurrection of His body and its open demonstration as the monument of His victory? How could the destruction of death have been manifested at all, had not the Lord's body been raised? But if anyone finds even this insufficient, let him find proof of what has been said in present facts. Dead men cannot take effective action; their power of influence on others lasts only till the grave. Deeds and actions that energise others belong only to the living. Well, then, look at the facts in this case. The Saviour is working mightily among men, every day He is invisibly persuading numbers of people all over the world, both within and beyond the Greek-speaking world, to accept His faith and be obedient to His teaching. Can anyone, in face of this, still doubt that He has risen and lives, or rather that He is Himself the Life? Does a dead man prick the consciences of men, so that they throw all the traditions of their fathers to the winds and bow down before the teaching of Christ? If He is no longer active in the world, as He must needs be if He is dead, how is it that He makes the living to cease from their activities, the adulterer from his adultery, the murderer from murdering, the unjust from avarice, while the profane and godless man becomes religious? If He did not rise, but is still dead, how is it that He routs and persecutes and overthrows the false gods, whom unbelievers think to be alive, and the evil spirits whom they worship? For where Christ is named, idolatry is destroyed and the fraud of evil spirits is exposed; indeed, no such spirit can endure that Name, but takes to flight on sound of it. This is the work of One Who lives, not of one dead; and, more than that, it is the work of God. It would be absurd to say that the evil spirits whom He drives out and the idols which He destroys are alive, but that He Who drives out and destroys, and Whom they themselves acknowledge to be Son of God, is dead.

§ 31

In a word, then, those who disbelieve in the resurrection have no support in facts, if their gods and evil spirits do not drive away the supposedly dead Christ. Rather, it is He Who convicts them of being dead. We are agreed that a dead person can do nothing: yet the Saviour works mightily every day, drawing men to religion, persuading them to virtue, teaching them about immortality, quickening their thirst for heavenly things, revealing the knowledge of the Father, inspiring strength in face of death, manifesting Himself to each, and displacing the irreligion of idols; while the gods and evil spirits of the unbelievers can do none of these things, but rather become dead at Christ's presence, all their ostentation barren and void. By the sign of the cross, on the contrary, all magic is stayed, all sorcery confounded, all the idols are abandoned and deserted, and all senseless pleasure ceases, as the eye of faith looks up from earth to heaven. Whom, then, are we to call dead? Shall we call Christ dead, Who effects all this? But the dead have not the faculty to effect anything. Or shall we call death dead, which effects nothing whatever, but lies as lifeless and ineffective as are the evil spirits and the idols? The Son of God, "living and effective," [1] is active every day and effects the salvation of all; but death is daily proved to be stripped of all its strength, and it is the idols and the evil spirits who are dead, not He. No room for doubt remains, therefore, concerning the resurrection of His body.

Indeed, it would seem that he who disbelieves this bodily rising of the Lord is ignorant of the power of the Word and Wisdom of God. If He took a body to Himself at all, and made it His own in pursuance of His purpose, as we have shown that He did, what was the Lord to do with it, and what was ultimately to become of that body upon which the Word had descended? Mortal and offered to death on behalf of all as it was, it could not but die; indeed, it was for that very purpose that the Saviour had prepared it for Himself. But on the other hand it could not remain dead, because it had become the very temple of Life. It therefore died, as mortal, but lived again because of the Life within it; and its resurrection is made known through its works.

[1] Heb. iv. 12.

It is, indeed, in accordance with the nature of the invisible God that He should be thus known through His works; and those who doubt the Lord's resurrection because they do not now behold Him with their eyes, might as well deny the very laws of nature. They have ground for disbelief when works are lacking; but when the works cry out and prove the fact so clearly, why do they deliberately deny the risen life so manifestly shown? Even if their mental faculties are defective, surely their eyes can give them irrefragable proof of the power and Godhead of Christ. A blind man cannot see the sun, but he knows that it is above the earth from the warmth which it affords; similarly, let those who are still in the blindness of unbelief recognise the Godhead of Christ and the resurrection which He has brought about through His manifested power in others. Obviously He would not be expelling evil spirits and despoiling idols, if He were dead, for the evil spirits would not obey one who was dead. If, on the other hand, the very naming of Him drives them forth, He clearly is not dead; and the more so that the spirits, who perceive things unseen by men, would know if He were so and would refuse to obey Him. But, as a matter of fact, what profane persons doubt, the evil spirits *know*—namely that He is God; and for that reason they flee from Him and fall at His feet, crying out even as they cried when He was in the body, "We know Thee Who Thou art, the Holy One of God," and, "Ah, what have I in common with Thee, Thou Son of God? I implore Thee, torment me not." [1]

Both from the confession of the evil spirits and from the daily witness of His works, it is manifest, then, and let none presume to doubt it, that the Saviour has raised His

[1] *Cf.* Luke iv. 34 and Mark v. 7.

own body, and that He is very Son of God, having His being from God as from a Father, Whose Word and Wisdom and Whose Power He is. He it is Who in these latter days assumed a body for the salvation of us all, and taught the world concerning the Father. He it is Who has destroyed death and freely graced us all with incorruption through the promise of the resurrection, having raised His own body as its first-fruits, and displayed it by the sign of the cross as the monument to His victory over death and its corruption.

[The non-student reader may omit the next three chapters, and go on to the *Conclusion* on p. 95.]

CHAPTER VI

REFUTATION OF THE JEWS

§ 33

WE have dealt thus far with the Incarnation of our Saviour, and have found clear proof of the resurrection of His Body and His victory over death. Let us now go further and investigate the unbelief and the ridicule with which Jews and Gentiles respectively regard these same facts. It seems that in both cases the points at issue are the same, namely the unfittingness or incongruity (as it seems to them) alike of the cross and of the Word's becoming man at all. But we have no hesitation in taking up the argument against these objectors, for the proofs on our side are extremely clear.

First, then, we will consider the Jews. Their unbelief has its refutation in the Scriptures which even themselves read; for from cover to cover the inspired Book clearly teaches these things both in its entirety and in its actual words. Prophets foretold the marvel of the Virgin and of the Birth from her, saying, "Behold, a virgin shall conceive and bear a son, and they shall call his name *Emmanuel*, which means *God is with us*."[1] And Moses, that truly great one in whose word the Jews trust so implicitly, he also recognised the importance and truth of the matter. He puts it thus: "There shall arise a star from Jacob and a man from Israel, and he shall break in pieces the rulers of Moab."[2] And, again, "How lovely are thy dwellings, O Jacob, thy tents, O Israel! Like woodland valleys they give shade, and like parks by rivers, like tents which the Lord has pitched, like cedar-trees by streams. There shall come forth a Man from among his seed, and he shall rule over many peoples."[3] And, again, Isaiah says, "Before the Babe shall be old enough to call father or mother, he shall take the power of Damascus and the spoils of Samaria from under the eyes of the king of Assyria."[4] These words, then, foretell that a Man shall appear. And Scripture proclaims further that He that is to come is Lord of all. These are the words, "Behold, the Lord sitteth on an airy cloud and shall come into Egypt, and the man-made images of Egypt shall be shaken."[5] And it is from Egypt also that the Father calls him back, saying, "Out of Egypt have I called My Son."[6]

§ 34

Moreover, the Scriptures are not silent even about His death. On the contrary, they refer to it with the utmost clearness. They have not feared to speak also of the cause of it. He endures it, they say, not for His own sake, but for the sake of bringing immortality and salvation to all, and they record also the plotting of the Jews against Him and all the indignities which He suffered at their hands. Certainly nobody who reads the Scriptures can plead ignorance of the facts as an excuse for error! There is

[1] Isaiah vii. 14. [2] Numbers xxiv. 17. [3] Numbers xxiv. 5-7.
[4] Isaiah viii. 4. [5] Isaiah xix. 1. [6] Hosea xi. 1.

65

this passage, for instance: "A man that is afflicted and knows how to bear weakness, for His face is turned away. He was dishonoured and not considered, He bears our sins and suffers for our sakes. And we for our part thought Him distressed and afflicted and ill-used; but it was for our sins that He was wounded and for our lawlessness that He was made weak. Chastisement for our peace was upon Him, and by His bruising we are healed."[1] O marvel at the love of the Word for men, for it is on our account that He is dishonoured, so that we may be brought to honour. "For all we," it goes on, "have strayed like sheep, man has strayed from his path, and the Lord has given Him up for our sins; and He Himself did not open His mouth at the ill-treatment. Like a sheep He was led to slaughter, and as a lamb is dumb before its shearer, so He opened not His mouth; in His humiliation His judgment was taken away."[2] And then Scripture anticipates the surmises of any who might think from His suffering thus that He was just an ordinary man, and shows what power worked in His behalf. "Who shall declare of what lineage He comes?" it says, "for His life is exalted from the earth. By the lawlessnesses of the people was He brought to death, and I will give the wicked in return for His burial and the rich in return for His death. For He did no lawlessness, neither was deceit found in His mouth. And the Lord wills to heal Him of His affliction."[3]

§ 35

You have heard the prophecy of His death, and now, perhaps, you want to know what indications there are about the cross. Even this is not passed over in silence: on the contrary, the sacred writers proclaim it with the utmost plainness. Moses foretells it first, and that right loudly, when he says, "You shall see your Life hanging

[1] Isaiah liii. 3-5.　　[2] Isaiah liii. 6-8.　　[3] Isaiah liii. 8-10.

before your eyes, and shall not believe." [1] After him the prophets also give their witness, saying, "But I as an innocent lamb brought to be offered was yet ignorant of it. They plotted evil against Me, saying, 'Come, let us cast wood into His bread, and wipe Him out from the land of the living." [2] And, again, "They pierced My hands and My feet, they counted all My bones, they divided My garments for themselves and cast lots for My clothing." [3] Now a death lifted up and that takes place on wood can be none other than the death of the cross; moreover, it is only in that death that the hands and feet are pierced. Besides this, since the Saviour dwelt among men, all nations everywhere have begun to know God; and this too Holy Writ expressly mentions. "There shall be the Root of Jesse," it says, "and he who rises up to rule the nations, on Him nations shall set their hope." [4]

These are just a few things in proof of what has taken place; but indeed all Scripture teems with disproof of Jewish unbelief. For example, which of the righteous men and holy prophets and patriarchs of whom the Divine Scriptures tell ever had his bodily birth from a virgin only? Was not Abel born of Adam, Enoch of Jared, Noah of Lamech, Abraham of Terah, Isaac of Abraham, and Jacob of Isaac? Was not Judah begotten by Jacob and Moses and Aaron by Ameram? Was not Samuel the son of Elkanah, David of Jesse, Solomon of David, Hezekiah of Ahaz, Josiah of Amon, Isaiah of Amos, Jeremiah of Hilkiah and Ezekiel of Buzi? Had not each of these a father as author of his being? So who is He that is born of a virgin only, that sign of which the prophet makes so much? Again, which of all those people had his birth announced to the world by a star in the heavens? When Moses was born his parents hid him. David was unknown even in his own neighbourhood, so that mighty

[1] Deut. xxviii. 66.   [2] Jer. xi. 19.
[3] Psalm xxii. 16-18.   [4] Isaiah xi. 10,

67

Samuel himself was ignorant of his existence and asked whether Jesse had yet another son. Abraham again became known to his neighbours as a great man only after his birth. But with Christ it was otherwise. The witness to His birth was not man, but a star shining in the heavens whence He was coming down.

§ 36

Then, again, what king that ever was reigned and took trophies from his enemies before he had strength to call father or mother? Was not David thirty years old when he came to the throne and Solomon a grown young man? Did not Joash enter on his reign at the age of seven, and Josiah, some time after him, at about the same age, both of them fully able by that time to call father or mother? Who is there, then, that was reigning and despoiling his enemies almost before he was born? Let the Jews, who have investigated the matter, tell us if there was ever such a king in Israel or Judah—a king upon whom all the nations set their hopes and had peace, instead of being at enmity with him on every side! As long as Jerusalem stood there was constant war between them, and they all fought against Israel. The Assyrians oppressed Israel, the Egyptians persecuted them, the Babylonians fell upon them, and, strange to relate, even the Syrians their neighbours were at war with them. And did not David fight with Moab and smite the Syrians, and Hezekiah quail at the boasting of Sennacherib? Did not Amalek make war on Moses and the Amorites oppose him, and did not the inhabitants of Jericho array themselves against Joshua the son of Nun? Did not the nations always regard Israel with implacable hostility? Then it is worth enquiring who it is, on whom the nations are to set their hopes. Obviously there must be someone, for the prophet could not have told a lie. But did any of the holy prophets or of the early patriarchs die on the cross for the salvation of all? Was any of them wounded and killed for the healing of all? Did the idols of Egypt fall down before any righteous man or king that came there? Abraham came there certainly, but idolatry prevailed just the same; and Moses was born there, but the mistaken worship was unchanged.

§ 37

Again, does Scripture tell of anyone who was pierced in hands and feet or hung upon a tree at all, and by means of a cross perfected his sacrifice for the salvation of all? It was not Abraham, for he died in his bed, as did also Isaac and Jacob. Moses and Aaron died in the mountain, and David ended his days in his house, without anybody having plotted against him. Certainly he had been sought by Saul, but he was preserved unharmed. Again Isaiah was sawn asunder, but he was not hung on a tree. Jeremiah was shamefully used, but he did not die under condemnation. Ezekiel suffered, but he did so, not on behalf of the people, but only to signify to them what was going to happen. Moreover, all these even when they suffered were but men, like other men; but He Whom the Scriptures declare to suffer on behalf of all is called not merely man but Life of all, although in point of fact He did share our human nature. "You shall see your Life hanging before your eyes," they say, and "Who shall declare of what lineage He comes?" With all the saints we can trace their descent from the beginning, and see exactly how each came to be; but the Divine Word maintains that we cannot declare the lineage of Him Who is the Life. Who is it, then, of Whom Holy Writ thus speaks? Who is there so great that even the prophets foretell of Him such mighty things? There is indeed no one in the Scriptures at all, save the common Saviour of all, the Word of God, our

Lord Jesus Christ. He it is that proceeded from a virgin, and appeared as man on earth, He it is Whose earthly lineage cannot be declared, because He alone derives His body from no human father, but from a virgin alone. We can trace the paternal descent of David and Moses and of all the patriarchs. But with the Saviour we cannot do so, for it was He Himself Who caused the star to announce His bodily birth, and it was fitting that the Word, when He came down from heaven, should have His sign in heaven too, and fitting that the King of creation on His coming forth should be visibly recognised by all the world. He was actually born in Judaea, yet men from Persia came to worship Him. He it is Who won victory from His daemon foes and trophies from the idolaters even before His bodily appearing—namely, all the heathen who from every region have abjured the tradition of their fathers and the false worship of idols and are now placing their hope in Christ and transferring their allegiance to Him. The thing is happening before our very eyes, here in Egypt; and thereby another prophecy is fulfilled, for at no other time have the Egyptians ceased from their false worship save when the Lord of all, riding as on a cloud, came down here in the body and brought the error of idols to nothing and won over everybody to Himself and through Himself to the Father. He it is Who was crucified with the sun and moon as witnesses; and by His death salvation has come to all men, and all creation has been redeemed. He is the Life of all, and He it is Who like a sheep gave up His own body to death, His life for ours and our salvation.

§ 38

Yet the Jews disbelieve this. This argument does not satisfy them. Well, then, let them be persuaded by other things in their own oracles. Of whom, for instance, do the prophets say "I was made manifest to those who did not seek Me, I was found by those who had not asked for Me? I said, 'See, here am I,' to the nation that had not called upon My Name. I stretched out My hands to a disobedient and gainsaying people."[1] Who is this person that was made manifest, one might ask the Jews? If the prophet is speaking of himself, then they must tell us how he was first hidden, in order to be manifested afterwards. And, again, what kind of man is this prophet, who was not only revealed after being hidden, but also stretched out his hands upon the cross? Those things happened to none of those righteous men: they happened only to the Word of God Who, being by nature without body, on our account appeared in a body and suffered for us all. And if even this is not enough for them, there is other overwhelming evidence by which they may be silenced. The Scripture says, "Be strong, hands that hang down and feeble knees, take courage, you of little faith, be strong and do not fear. See, our God will recompense judgment, He Himself will come and save us. Then the eyes of blind men shall be opened and the ears of deaf men shall hear, and stammerers shall speak distinctly."[2] What can they say to this, or how can they look it in the face at all? For the prophecy does not only declare that God will dwell here, it also makes known the signs and the time of His coming. When God comes, it says, the blind will see, the lame will walk, the deaf will hear and the stammerers will speak distinctly. Can the Jews tell us when such signs occurred in Israel, or when anything of the kind took place at all in Jewry? The leper Naaman was cleansed, it is true, but no deaf man heard nor did any lame man walk. Elijah raised a dead person and so did Elisha; but no one blind from birth received his sight. To raise a dead person is a great thing indeed, but it is not such as the Saviour did. And surely,

---

[1] Isaiah lxv. 1, 2.   [2] Isaiah xxxv. 3-6.

since the Scriptures have not kept silence about the leper and the dead son of the widow, if a lame man had walked and a blind man had received his sight, they would have mentioned these as well. Their silence on these points proves that the events never took place. When therefore did these things happen, unless when the Word of God Himself came in the body? Was it not when He came that lame men walked and stammerers spoke clearly and men blind from birth were given sight? And the Jews who saw it themselves testified to the fact that such things had never before occurred. "Since the world began," they said, "it has never been heard of that anyone should open the eyes of a man born blind. If this Man were not from God, He could do nothing." [1]

§ 39

But surely they cannot fight against plain facts. So it may be that, without denying what is written, they will maintain that they are still waiting for these things to happen, and that the Word of God is yet to come, for that is a theme on which they are always harping most brazenly, in spite of all the evidence against them. But they shall be refuted on this supreme point more clearly than on any, and that not by ourselves but by the most wise Daniel, for he signifies the actual date of the Saviour's coming as well as His Divine sojourn in our midst. "Seventy weeks," he says, "are cut short upon thy people and upon the holy city, to make a complete end of sin and for sins to be sealed up and iniquities blotted out, and to make reconciliation for iniquity and to seal vision and prophet, and to anoint a Holy One of holies. And thou shalt know and understand from the going forth of the Word to answer,[2] and to build Jerusalem, until Christ the

[1] John ix. 32, 33.
[2] "Answer" is LXX misreading for Hebrew "restore."

Prince." [1] In regard to the other prophecies, they may possibly be able to find excuses for deferring their reference to a future time, but what can they say to this one? How can they face it at all? Not only does it expressly mention the Anointed One, that is the Christ, it even declares that He Who is to be anointed is not man only, but the Holy One of holies! And it says that Jerusalem is to stand till His coming, and that after it prophet and vision shall cease in Israel! David was anointed of old, and Solomon, and Hezekiah; but then Jerusalem and the place stood, and prophets were prophesying, Gad and Asaph and Nathan, and later Isaiah and Hosea and Amos and others. Moreover, those men who were anointed were called holy certainly, but none of them was called the Holy of holies. Nor is it any use for the Jews to take refuge in the Captivity, and say that Jerusalem did not exist then, for what about the prophets? It is a fact that at the outset of the Exile Daniel and Jeremiah were there, and Ezekiel and Haggai and Zechariah also prophesied.

§ 40

So the Jews are indulging in fiction, and transferring present time to future. When did prophet and vision cease from Israel? Was it not when Christ came, the Holy One of holies? It is, in fact, a sign and notable proof of the coming of the Word that Jerusalem no longer stands, neither is prophet raised up nor vision revealed among them. And it is natural that it should be so, for when He that was signified had come, what need was there any longer of any to signify Him? And when the Truth had come, what further need was there of the shadow? On His account only they prophesied continually, until such time as Essential Righteousness has come, Who was made

[1] Daniel ix. 24, 25.

73

the Ransom for the sins of all. For the same reason Jerusalem stood until the same time, in order that there men might premeditate the types before the Truth was known. So, of course, once the Holy One of holies had come, both vision and prophecy were sealed. And the kingdom of Jerusalem ceased at the same time, because kings were to be anointed among them only until the Holy of holies had been anointed. Moses also prophesies that the kingdom of the Jews shall stand until His time, saying, "A ruler shall not fail from Judah nor a prince from his loins, until the things laid up for him shall come and the Expectation of the nations Himself." [1] And that is why the Saviour Himself was always proclaiming "The law and the prophets prophesied until John." [2] So if there is still king or prophet or vision among the Jews, they do well to deny that Christ is come; but if there is neither king nor vision, and since that time all prophecy has been sealed and city and temple taken, how can they be so irreligious, how can they so flaunt the facts, as to deny Christ Who has brought it all about? Again, they see the heathen forsaking idols and setting their hopes through Christ on the God of Israel; why do they yet deny Christ Who after the flesh was born of the root of Jesse and reigns henceforward? Of course, if the heathen were worshipping some other god, and not confessing the God of Abraham and Isaac and Jacob and Moses, then they would do well to argue that God had not come. But if the heathen are honouring the same God Who gave the law to Moses and the promises to Abraham—the God Whose word too the Jews dishonoured, why do they not recognise or rather why do they deliberately refuse to see that the Lord of Whom the Scriptures prophesied has shone forth to the world and appeared to it in a bodily form? Scripture declares it repeatedly. "The Lord God has appeared to us," [3] and again, "He sent forth His Word

[1] Gen. xlix. 10.   [2] Matt. xi. 13.   [3] Psalm cxviii. 27.

74

and healed them." [1] And again, "It was no ambassador, no angel who saved us, but the Lord Himself." [2] The Jews are afflicted like some demented person who sees the earth lit up by the sun, but denies the sun that lights it up! What more is there for their Expected One to do when he comes? To call the heathen? But they are called already. To put an end to prophet and king and vision? But this too has already happened. To expose the God-denyingness of idols? It is already exposed and condemned. Or to destroy death? It is already destroyed. What then has not come to pass that the Christ must do? What is there left out or unfulfilled that the Jews should disbelieve so light-heartedly? The plain fact is, as I say, that there is no longer any king or prophet nor Jerusalem nor sacrifice nor vision among them; yet the whole earth is filled with the knowledge of God, and the Gentiles, forsaking atheism, are now taking refuge with the God of Abraham through the Word, our Lord Jesus Christ.

Surely, then, it must be plain even to the most shameless that the Christ has come, and that He has enlightened all men everywhere, and given them the true and divine teaching about His Father.

Thus the Jews may be refuted by these and other arguments from the Divine teaching.

CHAPTER VII

REFUTATION OF THE GENTILES

§ 41

WE come now to the unbelief of the Gentiles; and this is indeed a matter for complete astonishment, for they laugh at that which is no fit subject for mockery, yet fail to see the shame and ridiculousness of their own idols. But

---

[1] Psalm cvii. 20.   [2] Isaiah lxiii. 9.

the arguments on our side do not lack weight, so we will confute them too on reasonable grounds, chiefly from what we ourselves also see.

First of all, what is there in our belief that is unfitting or ridiculous? Is it only that we say that the Word has been manifested in a body? Well, if they themselves really love the truth, they will agree with us that this involved no unfittingness at all. If they deny that there is a Word of God at all, that will be extraordinary, for then they will be ridiculing what they do not know. But suppose they confess that there is a Word of God, that He is the Governor of all things, that in Him the Father wrought the creation, that by His providence the whole receives light and life and being, and that He is King over all, so that He is known by means of the works of His providence, and through Him the Father. Suppose they confess all this, what then? Are they not unknowingly turning the ridicule against themselves? The Greek philosophers say that the universe is a great body, and they say truly, for we perceive the universe and its parts with our senses. But if the Word of God is in the universe, which is a body, and has entered into it in its every part, what is there surprising or unfitting in our saying that He has entered also into human nature? If it were unfitting for Him to have embodied Himself at all, then it would be unfitting for Him to have entered into the universe, and to be giving light and movement by His providence to all things in it, because the universe, as we have seen, is itself a body. But if it is right and fitting for Him to enter into the universe and to reveal Himself through it, then, because humanity is part of the universe along with the rest, it is no less fitting for Him to appear in a human body, and to enlighten and to work through that. And surely if it were wrong for a part of the universe to have been used to reveal His Divinity to men, it would be much more wrong that He should be so revealed by the whole!

Take a parallel case. A man's personality actuates and quickens his whole body. If anyone said it was unsuitable for the man's power to be in the toe, he would be thought silly, because, while granting that a man penetrates and actuates the whole of his body, he denied his presence in the part. Similarly, no one who admits the presence of the Word of God in the universe as a whole should think it unsuitable for a single human body to be by Him actuated and enlightened.

But is it, perhaps, because humanity is a thing created and brought into being out of non-existence that they regard as unfitting the manifestation of the Saviour in our nature? If so, it is high time that they spurned Him from creation too; for it, too, has been brought out of non-being into being by the Word. But if, on the other hand, although creation is a thing that has been made, it is not unsuitable for the Word to be present in it, then neither is it unsuitable for Him to be in man. Man is a part of the creation, as I said before; and the reasoning which applies to one applies to the other. All things derive from the Word their light and movement and life, as the Gentile authors themselves say, "In Him we live and move and have our being." [1] Very well then. That being so, it is by no means unbecoming that the Word should dwell in man. So if, as we say, the Word has used that in which He is as the means of His self-manifestation, what is there ridiculous in that? He could not have used it had He not been present in it; but we have already admitted that He is present both in the whole and in the parts. What, then, is there incredible in His manifesting Himself through that in which He is? By His own power He enters completely into each and all, and orders them throughout ungrudgingly; and, had He so willed, He could have revealed Himself and His Father by means of

[1] See Acts xvii. 28.

sun or moon or sky or earth or fire or water. Had He done so, no one could rightly have accused Him of acting unbecomingly, for He sustains in one whole all things at once, being present and invisibly revealed not only in the whole, but also in each particular part. This being so, and since, moreover, He has willed to reveal Himself through men, who are part of the whole, there can be nothing ridiculous in His using a human body to manifest the truth and knowledge of the Father. Does not the mind of man pervade his entire being, and yet find expression through one part only, namely the tongue? Does anybody say on that account that Mind has degraded itself? Of course not. Very well, then, no more is it degrading for the Word, Who pervades all things, to have appeared in a human body. For, as I said before, if it were unfitting for Him thus to indwell the part, it would be equally so for Him to exist within the whole.

§ 43

Some may then ask, why did He not manifest Himself by means of other and nobler parts of creation, and use some nobler instrument, such as sun or moon or stars or fire or air, instead of mere man? The answer is this. The Lord did not come to make a display. He came to heal and to teach suffering men. For one who wanted to make a display the thing would have been just to appear and dazzle the beholders. But for Him Who came to heal and to teach the way was not merely to dwell here, but to put Himself at the disposal of those who needed Him, and to be manifested according as they could bear it, not vitiating the value of the Divine appearing by exceeding their capacity to receive it.

Moreover, nothing in creation had erred from the path of God's purpose for it, save only man. Sun, moon, heaven, stars, water, air, none of these had swerved from their order, but, knowing the Word as their Maker

78

and their King, remained as they were made. Men alone having rejected what is good, have invented nothings instead of the truth, and have ascribed the honour due to God and the knowledge concerning Him to daemons and men in the form of stones. Obviously the Divine goodness could not overlook so grave a matter as this. But men could not recognise Him as ordering and ruling creation as a whole. So what does He do? He takes to Himself for instrument a part of the whole, namely a human body, and enters into that. Thus He ensured that men should recognise Him· in the part who could not do so in the whole, and that those who could not lift their eyes to His unseen power might recognise and behold Him in the likeness of themselves. For, being men, they would naturally learn to know His Father more quickly and directly by means of a body that corresponded to their own and by the Divine works done through it; for by comparing His works with their own they would judge His to be not human but Divine. And if, as they say, it were unsuitable for the Word to reveal Himself through bodily acts, it would be equally so for Him to do so through the works of the universe. His being in creation does not mean that He shares its nature; on the contrary, all created things partake of His power. Similarly, though He used the body as His instrument, He shared nothing of its defect,[1] but rather sanctified it by His indwelling. Does not even Plato, of whom the Greeks think so much, say that the Author of the Universe, seeing it storm-tossed and in danger of sinking into the state of dissolution, takes his seat at the helm of the Life-force of the universe, and comes to the rescue and puts everything right? What, then, is there incredible in our saying that, mankind having gone astray, the Word descended upon it and was manifest as man, so that by His intrinsic goodness and His steersmanship He might save it from the storm?

[1] Literally, "He shared nothing of the things of the body."

79

§ 44

It may be, however, that, though shamed into agreeing that this objection is void, the Greeks will want to raise another. They will say that, if God wanted to instruct and save mankind, He might have done so, not by His Word's assumption of a body, but, even as He at first created them, by the mere signification of His will. The reasonable reply to that is that the circumstances in the two cases are quite different. In the beginning, nothing as yet existed at all; all that was needed, therefore, in order to bring all things into being, was that His will to do so should be signified. But once man was in existence, and things that were, not things that were not, demanded to be healed, it followed as a matter of course that the Healer and Saviour should align Himself with those things that existed already, in order to heal the existing evil. For that reason, therefore, He was made man, and used the body as His human instrument. If this were not the fitting way, and He willed to use an instrument at all, how otherwise was the Word to come? And whence could He take His instrument, save from among those already in existence and needing His Godhead through One like themselves? It was not things non-existent that needed salvation, for which a bare creative word might have sufficed, but man—man already in existence and already in process of corruption and ruin. It was natural and right, therefore, for the Word to use a human instrument and by that means unfold Himself to all.

You must know, moreover, that the corruption which had set in was not external to the body but established within it. The need, therefore, was that life should cleave to it in corruption's place, so that, just as death was brought into being in the body, life also might be engendered in it. If death had been exterior to the body, life might fittingly have been the same. But if death was within the body, woven into its very substance and dominating it as though completely one with it, the need was for Life to be woven into it instead, so that the body by thus enduing itself with life might cast corruption off. Suppose the Word had come outside the body instead of in it, He would, of course, have defeated death, because death is powerless against the Life. But the corruption inherent in the body would have remained in it none the less. Naturally, therefore, the Saviour assumed a body for Himself, in order that the body, being interwoven as it were with life, should no longer remain a mortal thing, in thrall to death, but as endued with immortality and risen from death, should thenceforth remain immortal. For once having put on corruption, it could not rise, unless it put on life instead; and besides this, death of its very nature could not appear otherwise than in a body. Therefore He put on a body, so that in the body He might find death and blot it out. And, indeed, how could the Lord have been proved to be the Life at all, had He not endued with life that which was subject to death? Take an illustration. Stubble is a substance naturally destructible by fire; and it still remains stubble, fearing the menace of fire which has the natural property of consuming it, even if fire is kept away from it, so that it is not actually burnt. But suppose that, instead of merely keeping the fire from it somebody soaks the stubble with a quantity of asbestos, the substance which is said to be the antidote to fire. Then the stubble no longer fears the fire, because it has put on that which fire cannot touch, and therefore it is safe. It is just the same with regard to the body and death. Had death been kept from it by a mere command, it would still have remained mortal and corruptible, according to its nature. To prevent this, it put on the incorporeal Word of God, and therefore fears neither death nor corruption any more, for it is clad with Life as with a garment and in it corruption is clean done away.

The Word of God thus acted consistently in assuming a body and using a human instrument to vitalise the body. He was consistent in working through man to reveal Himself everywhere, as well as through the other parts of His creation, so that nothing was left void of His Divinity and knowledge. For I take up now the point I made before, namely that the Saviour did this in order that He might fill all things everywhere with the knowledge of Himself, just as they are already filled with His presence, even as the Divine Scripture says, "The whole universe was filled with the knowledge of the Lord." [1] If a man looks up to heaven he sees there His ordering; but if he cannot look so high as heaven, but only so far as men, through His works he sees His power, incomparable with human might, and learns from them that He alone among men is God the Word. Or, if a man has gone astray among daemons and is in fear of them, he may see this Man drive them out and judge therefrom that He is indeed their Master. Again, if a man has been immersed in the element of water and thinks that it is God—as indeed the Egyptians do worship water—he may see its very nature changed by Him and learn that the Lord is Creator of all. And if a man has gone down even to Hades, and stands awestruck before the heroes who have descended thither, regarding them as gods, still he may see the fact of Christ's resurrection and His victory over death, and reason from it that, of all these, He alone is very Lord and God.

For the Lord touched all parts of creation, and freed and undeceived them all from every deceit. As St. Paul says, "Having put off from Himself the principalities and the powers, He triumphed on the cross," [2] so that no one could possibly be any longer deceived, but everywhere might find the very Word of God. For thus man, en-

[1] Isaiah xi. 9.   [2] Col. ii. 15.

closed on every side by the works of creation and every-where—in heaven, in Hades, in men and on the earth, beholding the unfolded Godhead of the Word, is no longer deceived concerning God, but worships Christ alone, and through Him rightly knows the Father.

On these grounds, then, of reason and of principle, we will fairly silence the Gentiles in their turn. But if they think these arguments insufficient to confute them, we will go on in the next chapter to prove our point from facts.

CHAPTER VIII

REFUTATION OF THE GENTILES—*continued*

§ 46

WHEN did people begin to abandon the worship of idols, unless it were since the very Word of God came among men? When have oracles ceased and become void of meaning, among the Greeks and everywhere, except since the Saviour has revealed Himself on earth? When did those whom the poets call gods and heroes begin to be adjudged as mere mortals, except when the Lord took the spoils of death and preserved incorruptible the body He had taken, raising it from among the dead? Or when did the deceitfulness and madness of daemons fall under contempt, save when the Word, the Power of God, the Master of all these as well, condescended on account of the weakness of mankind and appeared on earth? When did the practice and theory of magic begin to be spurned under foot, if not at the manifestation of the Divine Word to men? In a word, when did the wisdom of the Greeks become foolish, save when the true Wisdom of God revealed Himself on earth? In old times the whole world and every place in it was led astray by the worship of idols, and men thought the idols were the only gods that were. But now all over the world men are forsaking the fear of idols and taking refuge with Christ; and by worshipping Him as God they come through Him to know the Father also, Whom formerly they did not know. The amazing thing, moreover, is this. The objects of worship formerly were varied and countless; each place had its own idol and the so-called god of one place could not pass over to another in order to persuade the people there to worship him, but was barely reverenced even by his own. Indeed no! Nobody worshipped his neighbour's god, but every man had his own idol and thought that it was lord of all. But now Christ alone is worshipped, as One and the Same among all peoples everywhere; and what the feebleness of idols could not do, namely, convince even those dwelling close at hand, He has effected. He has persuaded not only those close at hand, but literally the entire world to worship one and the same Lord and through Him the Father.

§ 47

Again, in former times every place was full of the fraud of the oracles, and the utterances of those at Delphi and Dordona and in Boeotia and Lycia and Libya and Egypt and those of the Kabiri and the Pythoness were considered marvellous by the minds of men. But now, since Christ has been proclaimed everywhere, their madness too has ceased, and there is no one left among them to give oracles at all. Then, too, daemons used to deceive men's minds by taking up their abode in springs or rivers or trees or stones and imposing upon simple people by their frauds. But now, since the Divine appearing of the Word, all this fantasy has ceased, for by the sign of the cross, if a man will but use it, he drives out their deceits. Again, people used to regard as gods those who are mentioned

84

in the poets—Zeus and Kronos and Apollo and the heroes, and in worshipping them they went astray. But now that the Saviour has appeared among men, those others have been exposed as mortal men, and Christ alone is recognised as true God, Word of God, God Himself. And what is one to say about the magic that they think so marvellous? Before the sojourn of the Word, it was strong and active among Egyptians and Chaldaeans and Indians and filled all who saw it with terror and astonishment. But by the coming of the Truth and the manifestation of the Word it too has been confuted and entirely destroyed. As to Greek wisdom, however, and the philosophers' noisy talk, I really think no one requires argument from us; for the amazing fact is patent to all that, for all that they had written so much, the Greeks failed to convince even a few from their own neighbourhood in regard to immortality and the virtuous ordering of life. Christ alone, using common speech and through the agency of men not clever with their tongues, has convinced whole assemblies of people all the world over to despise death, and to take heed to the things that do not die, to look past the things of time and gaze on things eternal, to think nothing of earthly glory and to aspire only to immortality.

§ 48

These things which we have said are no mere words: they are attested by actual experience. Anyone who likes may see the proof of glory in the virgins of Christ, and in the young men who practise chastity as part of their religion, and in the assurance of immortality in so great and glad a company [1] of martyrs. Anyone, too, may put what we have said to the proof of experience in another way. In the very presence of the fraud of daemons and the

[1] Literally, "so great a *chorus* . . .", χορός being properly a band of dancers and singers.

imposture of the oracles and the wonders of magic, let him use the sign of the cross which they all mock at, and but speak the Name of Christ, and he shall see how through Him daemons are routed, oracles cease, and all magic and witchcraft is confounded.

Who, then, is this Christ and how great is He, Who by His Name and presence overshadows and confounds all things on every side, Who alone is strong against all and has filled the whole world with His teaching? Let the Greeks tell us, who mock at Him without stint or shame. If He is a man, how is it that one man has proved stronger than all those whom they themselves regard as gods, and by His own power has shown them to be nothing? If they call Him a magician, how is it that by a magician all magic is destroyed, instead of being rendered strong? Had He conquered certain magicians or proved Himself superior to one of them only, they might reasonably think that He excelled the rest only by His greater skill. But the fact is that His cross has vanquished all magic entirely and has conquered the very name of it. Obviously, therefore, the Saviour is no magician, for the very daemons whom the magicians invoke flee from Him as from their Master. Who is He, then? Let the Greeks tell us, whose only serious pursuit is mockery! Perhaps they will say that He, too, is a daemon, and that is why He prevailed. But even so the laugh is still on our side, for we can confute them by the same proofs as before. How could He be a daemon, Who drives daemons out? If it were only certain ones that He drove out, then they might reasonably think that He prevailed against them through the power of their Chief, as the Jews, wishing to insult Him, actually said. But since the fact is, here again, that at the mere naming of His Name all madness of the daemons is rooted out and put to flight, obviously the Greeks are wrong here, too, and our Lord and Saviour Christ is not, as they maintain, some daemonic power.

If, then, the Saviour is neither a mere man nor a magi-

86

cian, nor one of the daemons, but has by His Godhead confounded and overshadowed the opinions of the poets and the delusion of the daemons and the wisdom of the Greeks, it must be manifest and will be owned by all that He is in truth Son of God, Existent Word and Wisdom and Power of the Father. This is the reason why His works are no mere human works, but, both intrinsically and by comparison with those of men, are recognised as being superhuman and truly the works of God.

§ 49

What man that ever was, for instance, formed a body for himself from a virgin only? Or what man ever healed so many diseases as the common Lord of all? Who restored that which was lacking in man's nature or made one blind from birth to see? Aesculapius was deified by the Greeks because he practised the art of healing and discovered herbs as remedies for bodily diseases, not, of course, forming them himself out of the earth, but finding them out by the study of nature. But what is that in comparison with what the Saviour did when, instead of just healing a wound, He both fashioned essential being and restored to health the thing that He had formed? Hercules, too, is worshipped as a god by the Greeks because he fought against other men and destroyed wild animals by craft. But what is that to what the Word did, in driving away from men diseases and daemons and even death itself? Dionysus is worshipped among them, because he taught men drunkenness; yet they ridicule the true Saviour and Lord of all, Who taught men temperance.

That, however, is enough on this point. What will they say to the other marvels of His Godhead? At what man's death was the sun darkened and the earth shaken? Why, even to this day men are dying, and they did so also before that time. When did any such marvels happen in their case? Now shall we pass over the deeds done in His earthly body and mention those after His resurrection? Has any man's teaching, in any place or at any time, ever prevailed everywhere as one and the same, from one end of the earth to the other, so that his worship has fairly flown through every land? Again, if, as they say, Christ is man only and not God the Word, why do not the gods of the Greeks prevent His entering their domains? Or why, on the other hand, does the Word Himself dwelling in our midst make an end of their worship by His teaching and put their fraud to shame?

§ 50

Many before Him have been kings and tyrants of the earth, history tells also of many among the Chaldaeans and Egyptians and Indians who were wise men and magicians. But which of those, I do not say after his death, but while yet in this life, was ever able so far to prevail as to fill the whole world with his teaching and retrieve so great a multitude from the craven fear of idols, as our Saviour has won over from idols to Himself? The Greek philosophers have compiled many works with persuasiveness and much skill in words; but what fruit have they to show for this such as has the cross of Christ? Their wise thoughts were persuasive enough until they died; yet even in their life-time their seeming influence was counter-balanced by their rivalry with one another, for they were a jealous company and declaimed against each other. But the Word of God, by strangest paradox, teaching in meaner language, has put the choicest sophists in the shade, and by confounding their teachings and drawing all men to Himself He has filled His own assemblies. Moreover, and this is the marvellous thing, by going down as Man to death He has confounded all the sounding utterances of the wise men about the idols. For whose

88

death ever drove out daemons, or whose death did ever daemons fear, save that of Christ? For where the Saviour is named, there every daemon is driven out. Again, who has ever so rid men of their natural passions that fornicators become chaste and murderers no longer wield the sword and those who formerly were craven cowards boldly play the man? In a word, what persuaded the barbarians and heathen folk in every place to drop their madness and give heed to peace, save the faith of Christ and the sign of the cross? What other things have given men such certain faith in immortality as have the cross of Christ and the resurrection of His body? The Greeks told all sorts of false tales, but they could never pretend that their idols rose again from death: indeed it never entered their heads that a body could exist again after death at all. And one would be particularly ready to listen to them on this point, because by these opinions they have exposed the weakness of their own idolatry, at the same time yielding to Christ the possibility of bodily resurrection, so that by that means He might be recognised by all as Son of God.

§ 51

Again, who among men, either after his death or while yet living, taught about virginity and did not account this virtue impossible for human beings? But Christ our Saviour and King of all has so prevailed with His teaching on this subject that even children not yet of lawful age promise that virginity which transcends the law. And who among men has ever been able to penetrate even to Scythians and Ethiopians, or Parthians or Armenians or those who are said to live beyond Hyrcania, or even the Egyptians and Chaldaeans, people who give heed to magic and are more than naturally enslaved by the fear of daemons and savage in their habits, and to preach at all about virtue and self-control and against the worshipping

89

of idols, as has the Lord of all, the Power of God, our Lord Jesus Christ? Yet He not only preached through His own disciples, but also wrought so persuasively on men's understanding that, laying aside their savage habits and forsaking the worship of their ancestral gods, they learnt to know Him and through Him to worship the Father. While they were yet idolaters, the Greeks and Barbarians were always at war with each other, and were even cruel to their own kith and kin. Nobody could travel by land or sea at all unless he was armed with swords, because of their irreconcilable quarrels with each other. Indeed, the whole course of their life was carried on with the weapons, and the sword with them replaced the staff and was the mainstay of all aid. All this time, as I said before, they were serving idols and offering sacrifices to daemons, and for all the superstitious awe that accompanied this idol worship, nothing could wean them from that war-like spirit. But, strange to relate, since they came over to the school of Christ, as men moved with real compunction they have laid aside their murderous cruelty and are war-minded no more. On the contrary, all is peace among them and nothing remains save desire for friendship.

§ 52

Who, then, is He Who has done these things and has united in peace those who hated each other, save the beloved Son of the Father, the common Saviour of all, Jesus Christ, Who by His own love underwent all things for our salvation? Even from the beginning, moreover, this peace that He was to administer was foretold, for Scripture says, "They shall beat their swords into plough-shares and their spears into sickles, and nation shall not take sword against nation, neither shall they learn any more to wage war." [1] Nor is this by any means incredible.

[1] Isaiah ii. 4.

The barbarians of the present day are naturally savage in their habits, and as long as they sacrifice to their idols they rage furiously against each other and cannot bear to be a single hour without weapons. But when they hear the teaching of Christ, forthwith they turn from fighting to farming, and instead of arming themselves with swords extend their hands in prayer. In a word, instead of fighting each other, they take up arms against the devil and the daemons, and overcome them by their self-command and integrity of soul. These facts are proof of the Godhead of the Saviour, for He has taught men what they could never learn among the idols. It is also no small exposure of the weakness and nothingness of daemons and idols, for it was because they knew their own weakness that the daemons were always setting men to fight each other, fearing lest, if they ceased from mutual strife, they would turn to attack the daemons themselves. For in truth the disciples of Christ, instead of fighting each other, stand arrayed against daemons by their habits and virtuous actions, and chase them away and mock at their captain the devil. Even in youth they are chaste, they endure in times of testing and persevere in toils. When they are insulted, they are patient, when robbed they make light of it, and, marvellous to relate, they make light even of death itself, and become martyrs of Christ.

§ 53

And here is another proof of the Godhead of the Saviour, which is indeed utterly amazing. What mere man or magician or tyrant or king was ever able by himself to do so much? Did anyone ever fight against the whole system of idol-worship and the whole host of daemons and all magic and all the wisdom of the Greeks, at a time when all of these were strong and flourishing and taking everybody in, as did our Lord, the very Word of

God? Yet He is even now invisibly exposing every man's error, and single-handed is carrying off all men from them all, so that those who used to worship idols now tread them under foot, reputed magicians burn their books and the wise prefer to all studies the interpretation of the gospels. They are deserting those whom formerly they worshipped, they worship and confess as Christ and God Him Whom they used to ridicule as crucified. Their so-called gods are routed by the sign of the cross, and the crucified Saviour is proclaimed in all the world as God and Son of God. Moreover, the gods worshipped among the Greeks are now falling into disrepute among them on account of the disgraceful things they did, for those who receive the teaching of Christ are more chaste in life than they. If these, and the like of them, are human works, let anyone who will show us similar ones done by men in former time, and so convince us. But if they are shown to be, and are the works not of men but of God, why are the unbelievers so irreligious as not to recognise the Master Who did them? They are afflicted as a man would be who failed to recognise God the Artificer through the works of creation. For surely if they had recognised His Godhead through His power over the universe, they would recognise also that the bodily works of Christ are not human, but are those of the Saviour of all, the Word of God. And had they recognised this, as Paul says, "They would not have crucified the Lord of glory."[1]

§ 54

As, then, he who desires to see God Who by nature is invisible and not to be beheld, may yet perceive and know Him through His works, so too let him who does not see Christ with his understanding at least consider Him in His bodily works and test whether they be of man or God. If

[1] I Cor. ii. 8.

they be of man, then let him scoff; but if they be of God, let him not mock at things which are no fit subject for scorn, but rather let him recognise the fact and marvel that things divine have been revealed to us by such humble means, that through death deathlessness has been made known to us, and through the Incarnation of the Word the Mind whence all things proceed has been declared, and its Agent and Ordainer, the Word of God Himself. He, indeed, assumed humanity that we might become God. He manifested Himself by means of a body in order that we might perceive the Mind of the unseen Father. He endured shame from men that we might inherit immortality. He Himself was unhurt by this, for He is impassible and incorruptible; but by His own impassibility He kept and healed the suffering men on whose account He thus endured. In short, such and so many are the Saviour's achievements that follow from His Incarnation, that to try to number them is like gazing at the open sea and trying to count the waves. One cannot see all the waves with one's eyes, for when one tries to do so those that are following on baffle one's senses. Even so, when one wants to take in all the achievements of Christ in the body, one cannot do so, even by reckoning them up, for the things that transcend one's thought are always more than those one thinks that one has grasped.

As we cannot speak adequately about even a part of His work, therefore, it will be better for us not to speak about it as a whole. So we will mention but one thing more, and then leave the whole for you to marvel at. For, indeed, everything about it is marvellous, and wherever a man turns his gaze he sees the Godhead of the Word and is smitten with awe.

§ 55

The substance of what we have said so far may be summarised as follows. Since the Saviour's advent in our midst, not only does idolatry no longer increase, but it is getting less and gradually ceasing to be. Similarly, not only does the wisdom of the Greeks no longer make any progress, but that which used to be is disappearing. And daemons, so far from continuing to impose on people by their deceits and oracle-givings and sorceries, are routed by the sign of the cross if they so much as try. On the other hand, while idolatry and everything else that opposes the faith of Christ is daily dwindling and weakening and falling, see, the Saviour's teaching is increasing everywhere! Worship, then, the Saviour "Who is above all" and mighty, even God the Word, and condemn those who are being defeated and made to disappear by Him. When the sun has come, darkness prevails no longer; any of it that may be left anywhere is driven away. So also, now that the Divine epiphany of the Word of God has taken place, the darkness of idols prevails no more, and all parts of the world in every direction are enlightened by His teaching. Similarly, if a king be reigning somewhere, but stays in his own house and does not let himself be seen, it often happens that some insubordinate fellows, taking advantage of his retirement, will have themselves proclaimed in his stead; and each of them, being invested with the semblance of kingship, misleads the simple who, because they cannot enter the palace and see the real king, are led astray by just hearing a king named. When the real king emerges, however, and appears to view, things stand differently. The insubordinate impostors are shown up by his presence, and men, seeing the real king, forsake those who previously misled them. In the same way the daemons used formerly to impose on men, investing themselves with the honour due to God. But since the Word of God has been manifested in a body, and has made known to us His own Father, the fraud of the daemons is stopped and made to disappear; and men, turning their eyes to the

94

true God, Word of the Father, forsake the idols and come to know the true God.

Now this is proof that Christ is God, the Word and Power of God. For whereas human things cease and the fact of Christ remains, it is clear to all that the things which cease are temporary, but that He Who remains is God and very Son of God, the sole-begotten Word.

CHAPTER IX

CONCLUSION

§ 56

HERE, then, Macarius, is our offering to you who love Christ, a brief statement of the faith of Christ and of the manifestation of His Godhead to us. This will give you a beginning, and you must go on to prove its truth by the study of the Scriptures. They were written and inspired by God; and we, who have learned from inspired teachers who read the Scriptures and became martyrs for the Godhead of Christ, make further contribution to your eagerness to learn. From the Scriptures you will learn also of His second manifestation to us, glorious and divine indeed, when He shall come not in lowliness but in His proper glory, no longer in humiliation but in majesty, no longer to suffer but to bestow on us all the fruit of His cross—the resurrection and incorruptibility. No longer will He then be judged, but rather will Himself be Judge, judging each and all according to their deeds done in the body, whether good or ill. Then for the good is laid up the heavenly kingdom, but for those that practise evil outer darkness and the eternal fire. So also the Lord Himself says, "I say unto you, hereafter ye shall see the Son of Man

95

seated on the right hand of power, coming on the clouds of heaven in the glory of the Father." [1] For that Day we have one of His own sayings to prepare us, "Get ready and watch, for ye know not the hour in which He cometh." [2] And blessed Paul says, "We must all stand before the judgment seat of Christ, that each one may receive according as he practised in the body, whether good or ill." [3]

§ 57

But for the searching and right understanding of the Scriptures there is need of a good life and a pure soul, and for Christian virtue to guide the mind to grasp, so far as human nature can, the truth concerning God the Word. One cannot possibly understand the teaching of the saints unless one has a pure mind and is trying to imitate their life. Anyone who wants to look at sunlight naturally wipes his eye clear first, in order to make, at any rate, some approximation to the purity of that on which he looks; and a person wishing to see a city or country goes to the place in order to do so. Similarly, anyone who wishes to understand the mind of the sacred writers must first cleanse his own life, and approach the saints by copying their deeds. Thus united to them in the fellowship of life, he will both understand the things revealed to them by God and, thenceforth escaping the peril that threatens sinners in the judgment, will receive that which is laid up for the saints in the kingdom of heaven. Of that reward it is written: "Eye hath not seen nor ear heard, neither hath entered into the heart of man the things that God has prepared" [4] for them that live a godly life and love the God and Father in Christ Jesus our Lord, through Whom and with Whom be to the Father Himself, with the Son Himself, in the Holy Spirit, honour and might and glory to ages of ages. Amen.

[1] Matt. xxvi. 64.   [2] Matt. xxiv. 42.   [3] 2 Cor. v. 10.   [4] 1 Cor. ii. 9.

APPENDIX

THE LETTER OF ST. ATHANASIUS TO MARCELLINUS ON THE INTERPRETATION OF THE PSALMS

My dear Marcellinus,

YOUR steadfastness in Christ fills me with admiration. Not only are you bearing well your present trial, with its attendant suffering; you are even living under rule and, so the bearer of your letter tells me, using the leisure necessitated by your recent illness to study the whole body of the Holy Scriptures and especially the Psalms. Of every one of those, he says, you are trying to grasp the inner force and sense. Splendid! I myself am devoted to the Psalms, as indeed to the whole Bible; and I once talked with a certain studious old man, who had bestowed much labour on the Psalter, and discoursed to me about it with great persuasiveness and charm, expressing himself clearly too, and holding a copy of it in his hand the while he spoke. So I am going to write down for you the things he said.

SON, all the books of Scripture, both Old Testament and New, are inspired by God and useful for instruction, as the Apostle says; but to those who really study it the Psalter yields especial treasure. Each book of the Bible has, of course, its own particular message: the Pentateuch, for example, tells of the beginning of the world, the doings of the patriarchs, the exodus of Israel from Egypt, the giving of the Law, and the ordering of the tabernacle and the priesthood; Joshua, Judges, and Samuel describe the division of the inheritance, the acts of the judges, and the ancestry of David; Kings and Chronicles record the doings of the kings, Ezra the deliverance from exile, the return of the people, and the building of the temple and the city; the Prophets foretell the coming of the Saviour, put us in mind of the commandments, reprove transgressors, and for the Gentiles also have a special word. Each of these books, you see, is like a garden which grows one special kind of fruit; by contrast, the Psalter is a garden which, besides its special fruit, grows also some of those of all the rest. The creation, for instance, of which we read in Genesis, is spoken of in Psalm 19, "The heavens declare the glory of God: and the firmament showeth His handiwork," and again in 24, "The earth is the Lord's and the fullness thereof: the inhabited earth and all that dwell therein. He Himself laid the foundations of it on the seas." The exodus from Egypt, which Exodus, Numbers, and Deuteronomy record, is fitly sung in Psalms 87, 105, 106, and 114. "When Israel came out of Egypt," says this last, "the House of Jacob from among a foreign people, Judah became his holy place and Israel came under his authority." "He sent Moses His servant," Psalm 105 declares, "Aaron whom He had chosen. He showed them the words of His signs among them, and of His wonders in the land of Ham. Darkness He sent, and it was dark, and they were not obedient to His word. He turned their waters into blood and slew their fish: their land brought forth frogs, even in the king's apartments. He spake, and dog-flies came, and flies in all their quarters"; and so on, all through this Psalm and the next, we find the same things treated. As for the tabernacle and the priesthood, we have reference to them in Psalm 29, sung when the tabernacle was carried forth,[1] "Bring unto the Lord, ye sons of God, bring unto the Lord young rams, bring to the Lord glory and honour." The doings of Joshua, the son of Nun, and of the Judges also are mentioned, this time in Psalm 105, "They built them cities to dwell in and sowed fields and planted vineyards," for it was under Joshua that the promised land was given into their hands. And when we read repeatedly in this same Psalm, "They cried unto the Lord in their trouble and He saved them out of their distress," the period of the judges is

[1] This Psalm is headed in the Septuagint *A Psalm of David, when the Tabernacle went forth*.

referred to, for then it was that, when they cried to Him, He raised up judges to deliver them from their oppressors, each time the need arose. In the same way, Psalm 20 has the kings in mind when singing, "Some trust in chariots and some in horses, but we will gain glory by the Name of the Lord our God. They are brought down and fallen, but we are risen and stand upright." And Psalm 126 of the Gradual Psalms speaks of that which Ezra tells, "When the Lord turned the captivity of Sion, we became as those comforted"; and similarly Psalm 122, "I was glad when they said unto me, We will go into the House of the Lord. Our feet were set in thy gates, O Jerusalem! Jerusalem is built as a city that has fellowship within itself: thither the tribes go up, the tribes of the Lord, to testify to Israel."

You see, then, that all the subjects mentioned in the historical books are mentioned also in one Psalm or another; but when we come to the matters of which the Prophets speak we find that these occur in almost all. Of the coming of the Saviour and how, although He is God, He yet should dwell among us, Psalm 50 says, "God shall come openly, even our God, and He shall not keep silence"; and in Psalm 118 we read, "Blessed is he that cometh in the Name of the Lord! We have blessed you from the House of the Lord. God is the Lord, and He has given us light." That He Who comes is Himself the Father's Word, Psalm 107 thus sings, "He sent His Word and healed them, and rescued them out of all their distresses." For the God Who comes *is* this self-same Word Whom the Father sends, and of this Word Who is the Father's Voice, Whom well he knows to be the Son of God, the Psalmist sings again in 45, "My heart is inditing of a good Word"; and also in 110, "Out of the womb, before the dawn, have I begotten Thee." Whom else, indeed, should any call God's very Offspring, save His own Word and Wisdom? And he, who knows full well that it was through the Word that God said, "Let there be light, Let there be a firmament. Let there be all things," says again in Psalm 33, "By the Word of the Lord were the heavens made, and all the host of them by the Breath of His mouth." And, so far from being ignorant of the coming of

99

Messiah, he makes mention of it first and foremost in Psalm 45, "Thy throne, O God, is for ever and ever, a sceptre of justice is the sceptre of Thy kingdom. Thou hast loved righteousness and hated lawlessness: wherefore God, even thy God, hath anointed thee with the oil of gladness above thy fellows." Further, lest any one should think this coming was in appearance only, Psalm 87 shows that He Who was to come should both come as man and at the same time be He by Whom all things were made. "Mother Sion shall say, A man, a man indeed is born in her: and He himself, the Most Highest, founded her," it says; and that is equivalent to saying "The Word was God, all things were made by Him, and the Word became flesh." Neither is the Psalmist silent about the fact that He should be born of a virgin—no, he underlines it straight away in 45, which we were quoting but a moment since. "Harken, O daughter," he says, "and see and incline thine ear, and forget thine own people and thy father's house. For the King has desired thy beauty, and He is thy Lord." Is not this like what Gabriel said, "Hail, thou that art full of grace, the Lord is with thee"? For the Psalmist, having called Him the Anointed One, that is Messiah or Christ, forthwith declares His human birth by saying, "Harken, O daughter, and see"; the only difference being that Gabriel addresses Mary by an epithet, because he is of another race from her, while David fitly calls her his own daughter, because it was from him that she should spring.

Having thus shown that Christ should come in human form, the Psalter goes on to show that He can suffer in the flesh He has assumed. It is as foreseeing how the Jews would plot against Him that Psalm 2 sings, "Why do the heathen rage and peoples meditate vain things? The kings of the earth stood up and their rulers took counsel together against the Lord and against His Christ." And Psalm 22, speaking in the Saviour's own person, describes the manner of His death. "Thou has brought me into the dust of death, for many dogs have compassed me, the assembly of the wicked have laid siege to me. They pierced my hands and my feet, they numbered all my bones, they gazed and stared at me, they parted my garments among them and cast lots for my vesture." "They pierced my hands and my feet"— what else can that mean except the cross? and Psalms 88 and 69, again speaking in the Lord's own person, tell us further that He suffered these things, not for His own sake but for ours. "Thou has made Thy wrath to rest upon me," says the one; and the other adds, "I paid them things I never took." For He did not die as being Himself liable to death: He suffered *for us*, and bore in Himself the wrath that was the penalty of our transgression, even as Isaiah says, "Himself bore our sicknesses." So in Psalm 138 we say, "The Lord will make requital for me"; and in the 72nd the Spirit says, "He shall save the children of the poor and bring the slanderer low, for from the hand of the mighty He has set the poor man free, the needy man whom there was none to help."[1]

Nor is this all. The Psalter further indicates beforehand the bodily Ascension of the Saviour into heaven, saying in Psalm 24, "Lift up your gates, ye princes, and be ye lift up, ye everlasting doors, and the king of glory shall come in!" And again in 47, "God is gone up with a merry noise, the Lord with the voice of the trumpet." The Session also it proclaims, saying in Psalm 110, "The Lord said unto my Lord, Sit thou on My right hand, until I make thine enemies the footstool of thy feet." And Psalm 9 mentions also the coming destruction of the devil, crying, "Thou satest on Thy throne, Thou that judgest righteousness, Thou hast rebuked the heathen and the wicked one is destroyed." And that He should receive all judgement from the Father, this also the Psalter does not hide from us, but foreshows Him as coming to be the Judge of all in 72, "Give the King Thy judgements, O God, and Thy righteousness unto the King's Son, that He may judge Thy people in righteousness and Thy poor with justice." In Psalm 50 too we read, "He shall call the heaven from above, and the earth, that He may judge His people. And the heavens shall declare His righteousness, that God is Judge indeed." The 82nd like-

---

[1] Athanasius takes these last two quotations as referring to the Resurrection, although it is not named.

wise says, "God standeth in the assembly of gods, in the midst He judges gods." The calling of the Gentiles also is to be learnt from many passages in this same book, especially in these words of Psalm 47, "O clap your hands together, all ye Gentiles, shout unto God with the voice of triumph"; and again in the 72nd, "The Ethiopians shall fall down before Him, His enemies shall lick the dust. The kings of Tarsis and of the islands shall bring presents, the kings of Arabia and Saba shall offer gifts." All these things are sung of in the Psalter; and they are shown forth separately in the other books as well.

My old friend made rather a point of this, that the things we find in the Psalms about the Saviour are stated in the other books of Scripture too; he stressed the fact that one interpretation is common to them all, and that they have but one voice in the Holy Spirit.

Moreover, he went on, the opposite is true, to some extent; for, just as the Psalter includes the special subjects of all the other books, so also do they often contain something of the special feature of the Psalter. Moses, for example, writes a song; Isaiah does the same, and Habakkuk offers prayer in form of song. And in the same way in every book we see something alike of prophecy, of law-giving, and of history; for the same Spirit is on all and He, being by nature One and Indivisible, is given whole to each: yet is He diverse in His manifestations to mankind, and each one who is taught by and receives Him ministers the word according to the moment's need. Thus (as I said before) Moses is at times a prophet and a psalmist, and the Prophets on occasion both lay down laws (like "Wash you, make you clean. Wash clean your heart from wickedness, Jerusalem"), and also record history, as when Daniel relates the story of Susanna or Isaiah tells us about the Rab-shakeh and Sennacherib. Similarly the Psalter, whose special function is to utter songs, generalizes in song matters that are treated in detail in the other books, as I have shown you. It also even lays down laws at times, such as "Leave off from wrath and let go displeasure, incline thine heart from evil and do good. Seek peace and ensue it," as well as telling us the history of Israel's journey and prophesying the coming of the Saviour, as I said just now.

You see, then, that the grace of the one Spirit is common to every writer and all the books of Scripture, and differs in its expression only as need requires and the Spirit wills. Obviously, therefore, the only thing that matters is for each writer to hold fast unyieldingly the grace he personally has received and so fulfil perfectly his individual mission. And, among all the books, the Psalter has certainly a very special grace, a choiceness of quality well worthy to be pondered; for, besides the characteristics which it shares with others, it has this peculiar marvel of its own, that within it are represented and portrayed in all their great variety the movements of the human soul. It is like a picture, in which you see yourself portrayed and, seeing, may understand and consequently form yourself upon the pattern given. Else-where in the Bible you read only that the Law commands this or that to be done, you listen to the Prophets to learn about the Saviour's coming or you turn to the historical books to learn the doings of the kings and holy men; but in the Psalter, besides all these things, you learn about *yourself*. You find depicted in it all the movements of your soul, all its changes, its ups and downs, its failures and recoveries. Moreover, whatever your particular need or trouble, from this same book you can select a form of words to fit it, so that you do not merely hear and then pass on, but learn the way to remedy your ill. Prohibitions of evil-doing are plentiful in Scripture, but only the Psalter tells you how to obey these orders and refrain from sin. Repentance, for example, is enjoined repeatedly; but to repent means to leave off sinning, and it is the Psalms that show you how to set about repenting and with what words your penitence may be expressed. Again, Saint Paul says, "Tribulation worketh endurance, and endurance experience, and experience hope, and hope maketh not ashamed"; but it is in the Psalms that we find written and described how afflictions should be borne, and what the afflicted ought to say, both at the time and when his troubles cease: the whole process of his testing is set forth in them and we are shown exactly with what words to voice our hope in God. Or take the command-ment, "In everything give thanks." The Psalms not only exhort us to be thankful, they also provide us with fitting words to say. We are told, too, by other writers that all who would live godly in Christ must suffer persecution; and here again the Psalms supply words with which both those who flee persecution and those who suffer under it may suitably address themselves to God, and it does the same for those who have been rescued from it. We are bidden elsewhere in the Bible also to bless the Lord and to acknow-ledge Him: here in the Psalms we are shown the way to do it, and with what sort of words His majesty may meetly be confessed. In fact, under all the circumstances of life, we shall find that these divine songs suit ourselves and meet our own souls' need at every turn.

And herein is yet another strange thing about the Psalms. In the other books of Scripture we read or hear the words of holy men as belonging only to those who spoke them, not at all as though they were our own; and in the same way the doings there narrated are to us material for wonder and examples to be followed, but not in any sense things we have done ourselves. With this book, however, though one does read the prophecies about the Saviour in that way, with reverence and with awe, in the case of all the other Psalms it is as though it were one's own words that one read; and any one who hears them is moved at heart, as though they voiced for him his deepest thoughts. To make this clear and, like Saint Paul not fearing somewhat to repeat ourselves, let us take some examples. The patriarchs spoke many things, all fitting to themselves; Moses also spoke, and God answered; Elijah and Elisha, seated on Mount Carmel, called upon the Lord and said, "The Lord liveth, before Whom I stand.[1] And the other prophets, while speaking specially about the Saviour, addressed themselves also at times to Israel or to the heathen. Yet no one would ever

[1] See for Elijah I Kings 18: 15, 19, and for Elisha II Kings 2: 25 and 3: 14.

speak the patriarchs' words as though they were his own, or dare to imitate the utterance of Moses or use the words of Abraham concerning the great Isaac, or about Ishmael and the home-born slave, as though they were his own, even though like necessity oppressed him. Neither, if any man suffer with those that suffer or be gripped with desire of some better thing, would he ever say as Moses said, "Show me Thyself," or "If Thou remittest their sin, then remit it; but if not, then blot me out of Thy book that Thou hast written." No more would any one use the prophets' words of praise or blame as though they were his own, or say, "The Lord lives, in Whose sight I stand to-day." For he who reads those books is clearly reading not his own words but those of holy men and other people about whom they write; but the marvel with the Psalter is that, barring those prophecies about the Saviour and some about the Gentiles, the reader takes all its words upon his lips as though they were his own, and each one sings the Psalms as though they had been written for his special benefit, and takes them and recites them, not as though someone else were speaking or another person's feelings being described, but as himself speaking of himself, offering the words to God as his own heart's utterance, just as though he himself had made them up. Not as the words of the patriarchs or of Moses and the other prophets will he reverence these: no, he is bold to take them as his own and written for his very self. Whether he has kept the Law or whether he has broken it, it is his own doings that the Psalms describe; every one is bound to find his very self in them and, be he faithful soul or be he sinner, each reads in them descriptions of himself.

It seems to me, moreover, that because the Psalms thus serve him who sings them as a mirror, wherein he sees himself and his own soul, he cannot help but render them in such a manner that their words go home with equal force to those who hear him sing, and stir them also to a like reaction. Sometimes it is repentance that is generated in this way, as by the conscience-stirring words of Psalm 51; another time, hearing how God helps those who hope and trust in Him, the listener too rejoices and begins to render thanks, as though that gracious help already were his own. Psalm 3, to take another instance, a man will sing, bearing his own afflictions in his mind; Psalms 11 and 12 he will use as the expression of his own faith and prayer; and singing the 54th, the 56th, the 57th, and the 142nd, it is not as though someone else were being persecuted but out of his own experience that he renders praise to God. And every other Psalm is spoken and composed by the Spirit in the selfsame way: just as in a mirror, the movements of our own souls are reflected in them and the words are indeed our very own, given us to serve both as a reminder of our changes of condition and as a pattern and model for the amendment of our lives.

This is the further kindness of the Saviour that, having become man for our sake, He not only offered His own body to death on our behalf, that He might redeem all from death, but also, desiring to display to us His own heavenly and perfect way of living, He expressed this in His very self. It was as knowing how easily the devil might deceive us, that He gave us, for our peace of mind, the pledge of His own victory that He had won on our behalf. But He did not stop there: He went still further, and His own self performed the things He had enjoined on us. Every man therefore may both hear Him speaking and at the same time see in His behaviour the pattern for his own, even as He himself has bidden, saying, "Learn of Me, for I am meek and lowly of heart." Nowhere is more perfect teaching of virtue to be found than in the Lord's own life. Forbearance, love of men, goodness, courage, mercy, righteousness, all are found in Him; and in the same way no virtue will be lacking to him who fully contemplates this human life of Christ. It was as knowing this that Saint Paul said, "Be ye imitators of me, even as I myself am of Christ." The Greek legislators had indeed a great command of language; but the Lord, the true Lord of all, Who cares for all His works, did not only lay down precepts but also gave Himself as model of how they should be carried out, for all who would to know and imitate. And therefore, *before* He came among us, He sketched the likeness of this perfect life for us in words, in

106

this same book of Psalms; in order that, just as He revealed Himself in flesh to be the perfect, heavenly Man, so in the Psalms also men of good-will might see the pattern life portrayed, and find therein the healing and correction of their own.

Briefly, then, if indeed any more is needed to drive home the point, the whole divine Scripture is the teacher of virtue and true faith, but the Psalter gives a picture of the spiritual life. And, just as one who draws near to an earthly king observes the formalities in regard to dress and bearing and the correct forms of words lest, transgressing in these matters, he be deemed a boor, so he who seeks to live the good life and learn about the Saviour's conduct in the body is by the reading of this holy book first put in mind of his own soul's condition and then supplied with fit words for a suppliant's use. For it is a feature of this book that the Psalms which compose it are of many different sorts. Some such as 73, 78, 114, and 115, are narrative in form; some are hortatory, like 32, 97, and 103; some are prophetic, for example, 22, 45, 47, and 110; some, in whole or part, are prayers to God, as are 6, 16, 54, 102; some are confessions, notably the 51st, some denounce the wicked, like 14; while yet others, such as 8, 98, 117, 125, and many more, voice thanksgiving, praise, and jubilation, Psalm 66 alone of these having special reference to the Resurrection of the Lord. It is possible for us, therefore, to find in the Psalter not only the reflection of our own soul's state, together with precept and example for all possible conditions, but also a fit form of words wherewith to please the Lord on each of life's occasions, words both of repentance and of thankfulness, so that we fall not into sin; for it is not for our actions only that we must give account before the Judge, but also for our every idle word.

Suppose, then, for example, that you want to declare any one to be blessed; you find the way to do it in Psalm 1, and likewise in 32, 41, 112, 119, and 128. If you want to rebuke the conspiracy of the Jews against the Saviour, you have Psalm 2. If you are persecuted by your own family and opposed by many, say Psalm 3; and when you would give

thanks to God at your affliction's end, sing 4 and 75 and 116.
When you see the wicked wanting to ensnare you and you
wish your prayer to reach God's ears, then wake up early
and sing 5; and if you feel yourself beneath the cloud of His
displeasure, you can say 6 and 38. If any plot against you,
as did Ahithophel against David, and someone tells you of
it, sing Psalm 7, and put your trust in God Who will deliver
you.   Contemplating humanity's redemption and the
Saviour's universal grace, sing Psalm 8 to the Lord; and
with this same Psalm or the 19th you may thank Him for the
vintage. For victory over the enemy and the saving of
created things, take not glory to yourself but, knowing
that it is the Son of God Who has thus brought things
to a happy issue, say to Him Psalm 9; and, if any wishes
to alarm you, the 11th, still trusting in the Lord. When
you see the boundless pride of many, and evil passing
great, so that among men (so it seems) no holy thing
remains, take refuge with the Lord and say Psalm 12. And
if this state of things be long drawn out, be not faint-hearted,
as though God had forgotten you, but call upon Him with
Psalm 27. Should you hear others blaspheme the providence of God, do not join with them in their profanity but
intercede with God, using the 14th and the 53rd. And if, by
way of contrast, you want to learn what sort of person is
citizen of heaven's kingdom, then sing Psalm 15. When,
again, you need to pray against your enemies and those who
straiten you, Psalms 17, 86, 88, and 140 will all meet your
need; and if you want to know how Moses prayed, you
have the 90th.[1] When you have been delivered from these
enemies and oppressors, then sing Psalm 18; and when you
marvel at the order of creation and God's good providence
therein and at the holy precepts of the Law, 19 and 24 will
voice your prayer; while 20 will give you words to comfort
and to pray with others in distress. When you yourself are
fed and guided by the Lord and, seeing it, rejoice, the 23rd
awaits you. Do enemies surround you? Then lift up your
heart to God and say Psalm 25, and you will surely see the
sinners put to rout. If they persist, their murderous intent

[1] Headed in the Septuagint, *A Prayer of Moses, Man of God.*

unslaked, then let man's judgement go and pray to God, the Only Righteous, that He alone will judge according unto right, using Psalms 26 and 35 and 43. If your foes press yet harder and become a veritable host, that scorns you as not yet anointed,[1] be not afraid, but sing again Psalm 27. Pay no attention either to the weakness of your own humanity or to the brazenness of their attack, but cry unceasingly on God, using Psalm 28. And when you want the right way of approach to God in thankfulness, with spiritual understanding sing Psalm 29. And finally, when you dedicate your home, that is your soul in which you receive the Lord and the house of your senses, in which corporeally your spirit dwells, give thanks and say the 30th and, from the Gradual Psalms, the 127th. Again, when you find yourself hated and persecuted by all your friends and kinsfolk because of your faith in Christ, do not despair on this account nor be afraid of them, but go apart and, looking to the future, sing Psalm 31. And when you see people baptized and ransomed from this evil world, be filled with wonder at the love of God for men, and in thanksgiving for them sing the 32nd. And whenever a number of you want to sing together, being all good and upright men, then use the 33rd. When you have fallen among enemies but have escaped by wise refusal of their evil counsel, then also gather holy men together and sing with them the 34th. And when you see how zealous are the lawless in their evil-doing, think not the evil is innate in them, as some false teachers say, but read Psalm 36 and you will see they are themselves the authors of their sin. And if you see these same wicked men trying, among other evils, to attack the weak and you wish to warn their victims to pay no heed to them, nor envy them, since they will soon be brought to nought, both to yourself and others say the 37th. When, on the other hand, it is your own safety that is in question, by reason of the enemy's attacks, and you wish to bestir yourself against him, say the 39th; and if, when he

[1] The title of Psalm 27 in the Greek is *Of David, before he was anointed.* The Christian reference is to chrismation, i.e., Confirmation, which was conferred as part of the same rite with Baptism in the early Church.

attacks, you then endure afflictions, and wish to learn the value of endurance, sing Psalm 40. When you see people in poverty, obliged to beg their bread, and you want to show them pity, you can applaud those who have already helped them and incite others to like works of mercy by using 41. Then again, if you are aflame with longing for God, be not disturbed at the reviling of your enemies but, knowing the immortal fruit that such desire shall bear, comfort your soul and ease your pains with hope in God, and say the 42nd. When you wish to recall in detail the loving-kindnesses which God showed to the fathers, both in their exodus from Egypt and in the wilderness, and to reflect how good God is and how ungrateful are men, you have the 44th, the 78th, the 89th, the 105th, 106th, 107th, and also the 114th and 115th. And the 46th will supply your need when after deliverance from afflictions you flee to God, and want to give Him thanks and tell of all His loving mercy shown towards yourself.

But suppose now that you have sinned and, having been put to confusion, are repenting and begging for forgiveness, then you have the words of confession and repentance in Psalm 51. Or you have been slandered, perhaps, before an evil king, and you see the slanderer boasting of his deed: then go away and say Psalm 52. And when they persecute and slander you, as did the Ziphites and the strangers to King David, be not disturbed but with full confidence in God sing praise to Him, using Psalms 54 and 56. If still the persecution follows hard on you, and he who seeks your life enters (though he knows it not) the very cave in which you hide, still you must not fear; for even in such extremity as this you have encouragement in Psalm 57 and also in the 142nd. The plotter, it may be, gives orders that a watch be kept over your house, and yet you manage to escape; give thanks to God, then, and let Psalm 59 be written on your heart, as on a pillar, as a memorial of your deliverance. And if not only your enemies cast you in the teeth but those also whom you thought to be your friends reproach and slander you and hurt you sorely for a time, you can still call upon God for help, using Psalm 55. Against hypocrites and those who glory in appearances, say for their reproach the 58th. But against those whose enmity is such that they would even take away your life, you must simply oppose your own obedience to the Lord, having no fear at all but all the more submitting to His will as they grow fiercer in their rage, and your form of words for this will be the 62nd Psalm. Should persecution drive you to the desert, fear not as though you were alone in it, for God is with you, and there at daybreak you may sing to Him the 63rd. And if even there the fear of foes and their unceasing plots pursues you, be they never so many or so insistent in their search for you, still you must not yield; for the toy arrows of a child will be enough to wound them, while Psalms 64, 65, 70, and 71 are on your lips.

The 65th Psalm will meet your need, whenever you desire to sing praise to God: and if you want to teach any one about the Resurrection, sing the 66th. When asking mercy from the Lord, praise Him with the 67th. When you see wicked men enjoying prosperity and peace and good men in sore trouble, be not offended or disturbed at it but say Psalm 73. When God is angry with His people, you have wise words of comfort in Psalm 74. When you have occasion to testify concerning God, 9, 71, 75, 92, 105 to 108, 111, 118, 126, 136, and 138 all fit the case; and Psalm 76, when used intelligently, provides you with an answer for the heathen and the heretics, showing that the knowledge of God is not with them at all, but only in the Church. And when the enemy takes possession of your place of refuge, even though sorely harassed and afflicted, do not despair but pray: and when your crying has been heard, give thanks to God, using Psalm 77. And if they have profaned the house of God and slain the saints, throwing their bodies to the birds of prey, do not be crushed or frightened at such cruelty but, suffering with those that suffer it, plead you for them with God, using Psalm 79.

Psalms 81 and 95 are suitable if you want to sing on a festival, together with other servants of the Lord; and when the enemy once more muster round you, threatening God's House and joining forces against His holy ones, do not you be frightened of either their numbers or their strength, for you have a very anchor of hope available in Psalm 83. If, moreover, you behold the House of God and His eternal dwelling, and have a longing for them, as the Apostle had, then say the 84th; and when at length their anger is abated and you are free again, voice your thanksgiving in the 85th and in the 116th. To see the difference between the Church and schism and to confound schismatics, you can say 87. To encourage yourself and others in the fear of God and to show how fearless is the soul that hopes in Him, say 91. Do you want to give thanks on the Lord's Day? Then say the 24th; if on a Monday, then the 95th; and if on a Friday, your words of praise are in the 93rd, for it was when the Crucifixion was accomplished that the House of God was built, for all the enemy attempted to prevent it, so it is fitting we should sing on Friday a song of victory, such as that Psalm is. Psalm 96 is apt, if God's House has been captured and destroyed and then re-built; and when the land has rest from war and peace returns, sing that "The Lord is King" in 97. You want to sing on Wednesday? The Psalm then is 94; for it was on the fourth day from the Sabbath[1] that the Lord through His betrayal entered on His Passion, by which He should redeem us and by the which He triumphed gloriously. So when you read in the Gospel how on the Wednesday the Jews took counsel against the Lord, seeing Him thus boldly challenging the devil on our behalf, sing the words of this Psalm 94. And again, when you see the providence and power of God in all things and want to instruct others in His faith and obedience, get them first to say the 100th Psalm. And when you have yourself experienced His power in judgement (for always His justice is tempered by His mercy) the next Psalm will express your need.

If through the weakness of your nature and the strain of of life you find yourself at times downcast and poor, sing for your consolation Psalm 102, and use the two that follow it to lift your heart in thankful praise to God, as in and through

[1] This Psalm is headed in the Septuagint, *A Psalm of David for the fourth day from the Sabbath.*

all circumstances we should always do. Psalms 105, 107, 113, 117, 135, and 146 to 150 not only show the reasons why God should be praised, but tell you how to do it. Have you faith, as the Lord bade, and believe in the prayers you utter? Then say the 116th Psalm, from the tenth verse on. You feel that, like the Apostle, you can now press forward, forgetting all the things that lie behind? Then you have the fifteen Gradual Psalms for every step of your advance. Another time, perhaps, you find you have been led astray by others' arguments—well, then, the moment you perceive it, stop your sinning, sit down and weep, as they did of old by Babylon's waters, using the words of Psalm 137. Since it is precisely by being tempted that one's worth is proved, Psalm 139 will meet your need when you thank God for testing safely past. And if the enemy once more gets hold of you and you desire to be free, then say 140. For prayer and supplication, sing Psalms 5, 141 to 143, and 146. Has some Goliath risen up against the people and yourself? Fear not, but trust in God, as David did, and sing his words in Psalm 144. Then, marvelling at God's kindnesses to every one and mindful of His goodness to yourself and all, praise Him, again in David's words, with Psalm 105. You want to sing to Him? Use 96 and 98. If, weak as you are, you yet are chosen for some position of authority among the brethren, you must not be puffed up as though you were superior to them, but rather glorify the Lord Who chose you and sing Psalm 151,[1] which is especially the Psalm of David. And for Psalms in praise of God, having some of them the title *Alleluya*, you have all these, 105 to 107, 111 to 118, 135, 136, 146 to 150. If, again, you want to sing Psalms that speak especially about the Saviour, you will find something in almost all of them; but 45 and 110 relate particularly to His Divine Begetting from the Father and His coming in the flesh, while 22 and 69 foretell the holy cross, the grievous plots He bore and how great things He suffered for our sakes. The 3rd and 109th also display the snares and malice of the Jews and how Iscariot betrayed Him; 21, 50, and 72

[1] This Psalm is found in the Greek version only. A translation is given on page 43.

all set Him forth as Judge and foretell His Second Coming in the flesh to us; they also show the Gentiles' call. The 16th shows His resurrection from the dead, in flesh, the 24th and 47th His ascension into heaven. And in the four Psalms 93, 96, 98, and 99, all the benefits deriving to us from the Saviour's Passion are set forth together.

Such, then, is the character of the Book of Psalms, and such the uses to which it may be put, some of its number serving for the correction of individual souls, and many of them, as I said just now, foretelling the coming in human form of our Saviour Jesus Christ. But we must not omit to explain the reason why words of this kind should be not merely said, but rendered with melody and song; for there are actually some simple folk among us who, though they believe the words to be inspired, yet think the reason for singing them is just to make them more pleasing to the ear! This is by no means so; Holy Scripture is not designed to tickle the aesthetic palate, and it is rather for the soul's own profit that the Psalms are sung. This is so chiefly for two reasons. In the first place, it is fitting that the sacred writings should praise God in poetry as well as prose, because the freer, less restricted form of verse, in which the Psalms, together with the Canticles and Odes,[1] are cast, ensures that by them men should express their love to God with all the strength and power they possess. And, secondly, the reason lies in the unifying effect which chanting the Psalms has upon the singer. For to sing the Psalms demands such concentration of a man's whole being on them that, in doing it, his usual disharmony of mind and corresponding bodily confusion is resolved, just as the notes of several flutes are brought by harmony to one effect; and he is thus no longer to be found thinking good and doing evil, as Pilate did when, though saying "I find no cause of death in Him," he yet allowed the Jews to have their way; nor desiring evil though unable to achieve it, as did the elders in their sin against

[1] The reference is probably to the hymns in Exodus 15: 1–18, Deuteronomy 32: 1–43, and Habakkuk 3, which are called Odes in the Septuagint. Some other Old Testament hymns, e.g. the Song of Hannah and the Benedicite, may be included.

Susanna—or, for that matter, as does any man who abstains from one sin and yet desires another every bit as bad. And it is in order that the melody may thus express our inner spiritual harmony, just as the words voice our thoughts, that the Lord Himself has ordained that the Psalms be sung and recited to a chant.

Moreover, to do this beautifully is the heart's desire and joy, as it is written, "Is any among you happy? Let him sing!" And if there is in the words anything harsh, irregular or rough, the tune will smoothe it out, as in our own souls also sadness is lightened as we chant, "Why then art thou so heavy, O my soul, why dost thou trouble me?" and failure is acknowledged as one sings, "My feet were almost gone," and fear is braced by hope in singing, "The Lord is my helper, I will not fear what man can do to me."

Well, then, they who do not read the Scriptures in this way, that is to say, who do not chant the Divine Songs intelligently but simply please themselves, most surely are to blame, for praise is not befitting in a sinner's mouth. But those who do sing as I have indicated, so that the melody of the words springs naturally from the rhythm of the soul and her own union with the Spirit, *they* sing with the tongue and with the understanding also, and greatly benefit not themselves alone but also those who want to listen to them. So was it with the blessed David when he played to Saul: he pleased God and, at the same time, he drove from Saul his madness and his anger and gave back peace to his distracted spirit. In like manner, the priests by their singing contributed towards the calming of the people's spirits and helped to unite them with those who lead the heavenly choir. When, therefore, the Psalms are chanted, it is not from any mere desire for sweet music but as the outward expression of the inward harmony obtaining in the soul, because such harmonious recitation is in itself the index of a peaceful and well-ordered heart. To praise God tunefully upon an instrument, such as well-tuned cymbals, cithara, or ten-stringed psaltery, is, as we know, an outward token that the members of the body and the thoughts of the heart are, like the instruments themselves, in proper order and control, all of them together living and moving by the Spirit's cry and breath. And similarly, as it is written that "By the Spirit a man lives and mortifies his bodily actions," so he who sings well puts his soul in tune, correcting by degrees its faulty rhythm so that at last, being truly natural and integrated, it has fear of nothing, but in peaceful freedom from all vain imaginings may apply itself with greater longing to the good things to come. For a soul rightly ordered by chanting the sacred words forgets its own afflictions and contemplates with joy the things of Christ alone.

So then, my son, let whoever reads this Book of Psalms take the things in it quite simply as God-inspired; and let each select from it, as from the fruits of a garden, those things of which he sees himself in need. For I think that in the words of this book all human life is covered, with all its states and thoughts, and that nothing further can be found in man. For no matter what you seek, whether it be repentance and confession, or help in trouble and temptation or under persecution, whether you have been set free from plots and snares or, on the contrary, are sad for any reason, or whether, seeing yourself progressing and your enemy cast down, you want to praise and thank and bless the Lord, each of these things the Divine Psalms show you how to do, and in every case the words you want are written down for you, and you can say them as your own.

There is, however, one word of warning needed. No one must allow himself to be persuaded, by any arguments whatever, to decorate the Psalms with extraneous matter or make alterations in their order or change the words themselves. They must be sung and chanted with entire simplicity,[1] just as they are written, so that the holy men who gave them to us, recognizing their own words, may pray with us, yes and even more that the Spirit, Who spoke by the saints, recognizing the selfsame words that He inspired, may join us in them too. For as the saints' lives are lovelier than any others, so too their words are better than ever ours can be, and of much more avail, provided only they be

---

[1] ἀτεχνῶς. The Benedictine editor translates, *sine ullo artificio*. The nearest single English word is *artlessly*.

uttered from a righteous heart. For with these words they themselves pleased God, and in uttering them, as the Apostle says, "they subdued kingdoms, they wrought righteousness, they obtained promises, they stopped the mouths of lions, quenched the power of fire, escaped the edge of the sword, from weakness were made strong, waxed mighty in war, turned to flight armies of aliens, women received their dead by resurrection." Let each one, therefore, who recites the Psalms have a sure hope that through them God will speedily give ear to those who are in need. For if a man be in trouble when he says them, great comfort will he find in them; if he be tempted or persecuted, he will find himself abler to stand the test and will experience the protection of the Lord, Who always defends those who say these words. By them too a man will overthrow the devil and put the fiends to flight. If he have sinned, when he uses them he will repent; if he have not sinned, he will find himself rejoicing that he is stretching out towards the things that are before and, so wrestling, in the power of the Psalms he will prevail. Never will such a man be shaken from the truth, but those who try to trick and lead him into error he will refute; and it is no human teacher who promises us this, but the Divine Scripture itself. For God commanded Moses to write a great song and to teach the people, and him whom He had appointed leader He bade also to write Deuteronomy, to have it ever in his hand and to meditate unceasingly upon its words; because these are sufficient in themselves both to call men's minds to virtue and to bring help to any who ponder them sincerely. It is a certain fact that when Joshua, the son of Nun, entered the land of promise and saw the ordered ranks of the heathern and the Amorite kings all drawn up against him, in face of all these swords and weapons he read Deuteronomy in the ears of all and reminded them of the words of the Law, and then, having thus armed the people, he overcame the foe. King Josiah also, when the book was found,[1] and had been read through to all, no longer feared his enemies. And at any

[1] Does he mean Deuteronomy again? If so, he anticipates the modern critical view about Josiah's Law Book by nearly sixteen hundred years!

time when war was threatening Israel, the Ark in which the tables of the Law were kept was carried out before the host, and was sufficient help against any array, except when there was among those who bore it or elsewhere among the people any prevailing hypocrisy or sin, for faith and an honest state of mind are always necessary if the Law is to be an effectual ally in the fulfilment of man's vows.

And I have heard, said the old man, from wise men, that in old days in Israel they put daemons to flight by reading of the Scriptures only, and in the same way uncovered plots made by them against men.

For this reason he rebuked as being worthy of the utmost condemnation people who neglect the Scriptures, while making use of impressive words from other sources for the purposes of exorcism so-called. Those who did that were playing with the sacred words, he said, and offering themselves as laughing-stock to daemons, as did those Jews, the sons of Sceva, when they tried in that way to exorcise the man at Ephesus. On the other hand, daemons fear the words of holy men and cannot bear them; for the Lord Himself is in the words of Scripture and Him they cannot bear, as they showed when they cried out to Christ, "I pray you, torment me not before the time." In the same way Paul commanded the unclean spirits, and daemons were subject to the disciples. The hand of the Lord was on Elisha the prophet also, and he prophesied about the waters to three kings, when the minstrel played and sang according to His bidding.[1] So also is it with us to-day: if any one have at heart the interests of those who suffer, let him use these words, and he will both help the sufferers more and at the same time prove his own faith to be true and strong; thus God, perceiving it, will grant the suppliants perfect health. Well knew the holy Psalmist that, when he said in Psalm 119, "I

[1] See Kings II: 3.

will meditate in Thy judgements: and I will not forget Thy words"; and again, "Thy statutes were my songs in the place of my sojourning." For with these words they all worked out their own salvation, saying, "If Thy law were not my meditation, then had I perished in my humiliation." Paul also strengthened his disciple with like words, saying, "Ponder these things, abide in them, that thy progress may be manifest."

And so you too, Marcellinus, pondering the Psalms and reading them intelligently, with the Spirit as your guide, will be able to grasp the meaning of each one, even as you desire. And you will strive also to imitate the lives of those God-bearing saints who spoke them at the first.

PSALM 151

This Psalm is ascribed to David and is outside the number. When he slew Goliath in single combat.[1]

1 Little was I among my brethren : a younger brother in my father's house.

2 My hands, they made an instrument of music : my fingers, they prepared a psaltery.

3 And who shall bring back tidings to my master? : the Lord Himself, Himself gives ear.

4 Himself sent forth His messenger : and took me from among my father's sheep; and with the oil of His anointing He anointed me.

5 Comely my brethren were and tall : and yet they found not favour with the Lord.

6 But I, I sallied forth to meet the alien : and he reviléd me by all his idols.

7 But I drew forth the sword that was beside him : I cut his head off with it, and from the sons of Israel removed reproach.

[1] This heading is that given in the Septuagint.

Hymns on Paradise –
St Ephrem the Syrian
ISBN 0-88141-076-4

On Ascetical Life – St Isaac of Nineveh
ISBN 0-88141-077-2

On God and Man – The Theological
Poetry of St Gregory of Nazianzus
ISBN 0-88141-220-1

On Marriage and Family Life –
St John Chrysostom
ISBN 0-913836-86-9

On Pascha – Melito of Sardis
ISBN 0-88141-217-1

On the Apostolic Preaching –
St Irenaeus
ISBN 0-88141-174-4

On the Apostolic Tradition –
Hippolytus
ISBN 0-88141-233-3

On the Christian Sacraments –
St Cyril of Jerusalem
ISBN 0-913836-39-7

On the Divine Images –
St John of Damascus
ISBN 0-913836-62-1

On the Divine Liturgy – St Germanus
ISBN 0-88141-038-1

On the Dormition –
Early Patristic Homilies
ISBN 0-88141-177-9

On the Holy Icons –
St Theodore the Studite
ISBN 0-913836-76-1

On the Holy Spirit – St Basil the Great
ISBN 0-913836-74-5

On the Incarnation – St Athanasius
ISBN 0-913836-40-0

On the Mother of God – Jacob of Serug
ISBN 0-88141-184-1

On the Mystical Life, vol. 1 –
St Symeon the New Theologian
ISBN 0-88141-142-6

On the Mystical Life, vol. 2 –
St Symeon the New Theologian
ISBN 0-88141-143-4

On the Mystical Life, vol. 3 –
St Symeon the New Theologian
ISBN 0-88141-144-2

On the Priesthood –
St John Chrysostom
ISBN 0-913836-38-9

On the Soul and Resurrection –
St Gegory of Nyssa
ISBN 0-88141-120-5

On the Unity of Christ –
St Cyril of Alexandria
ISBN 0-88141-133-7

On Wealth and Poverty –
St John Chrysostom
ISBN 0-88141-039-X

On God and Christ –
St Gregory of Nazianzus
ISBN 0-88141-240-6

*Three Treatises on the Divine
Images* – St John of Damascus
ISBN 0-88141-245-7

*On the Cosmic Mystery of Jesus
Christ* – St Maximus the Confessor
ISBN 0-88141-249-X

Letters from the Desert –
Barsanuphius and John
ISBN 0-88141-254-6

On the Lord's Prayer –
Tertullian, Cyprian, Origen
ISBN 0-88141-261-9

Four Desert Fathers –
Pambo, Evagrius, Macarius of Egypt,
and Macarius of Alexandria
ISBN 0-88141-256-2

Saint Macarius the Spiritbearer –
Coptic Texts
ISBN 0-88141-257-0

On the Human Condition –
St Basil the Great
ISBN 0-88141-294-5

ST VLADIMIR'S SEMINARY PRESS
575 Scarsdale Rd., Crestwood, New York 10707-1699
1-800-204-2665 • www.svspress.com